# Our Changing
# EARTH

BY THOMAS Y. CANBY

Prepared by the Book Division
National Geographic Society, Washington, D.C.

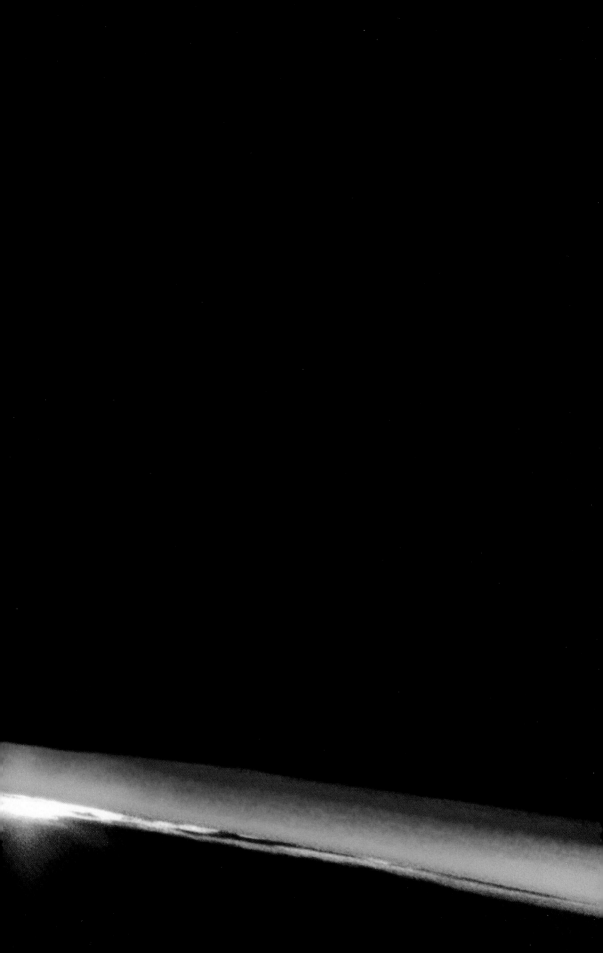

# OUR CHANGING EARTH

*By* Thomas Y. Canby

*Published by* The National Geographic Society
Gilbert M. Grosvenor,
*President and Chairman of the Board*
Michela A. English, *Senior Vice President*

*Prepared by The Book Division*
William R. Gray, *Vice President and Director*
Margery G. Dunn, Charles Kogod,
*Assistant Directors*

*Staff for this Book*
Margaret Sedeen, *Managing Editor*
Greta Arnold, *Illustrations Editor*
Suez B. Kehl, *Art Director*
Susan C. Eckert, Kimberly A. Kostyal,
Anne E. Withers, *Researchers*
Richard M. Crum, Edward Lanouette,
*Picture Legend Writers*

Sandra F. Lotterman, *Editorial Assistant*
Elizabeth G. Jevons, Artemis S. Lampathakis,
*Illustrations Assistants*

Lewis R. Bassford,
*Production Project Manager*
Timothy H. Ewing, H. Robert Morrison,
Richard S. Wain,
*Production*

Karen F. Edwards, Peggy J. Oxford,
Teresita Cóquia Sison, *Staff Assistants*

*Manufacturing and Quality Management*
George V. White, *Director,*
John T. Dunn, *Associate Director*
Vincent P. Ryan, *Manager,*
R. Gary Colbert

Anne K. McCain, *Indexer*

Library of Congress CIP Data: page 199

PAGE 1: *The aurora borealis shimmers across the northern sky, its glow sparked when solar wind particles hit the upper atmosphere.*

PAGES 2-3: *Ignited by a setting sun, Earth's atmosphere shines as a thin blue line of life in this view from a Soviet spacecraft.*

*Earth, sea, and sky merge as a pellucid playground for starfish in the tropical waters off Belize, in the Caribbean.*

*Thomson's gazelles graze Tanzania's
Serengeti Plain under a sky full of promise—
summer rains have come to rejuvenate
East Africa's parched grasslands.*

**S**pitting out sawdust as red as blood, the chain saw sank into the flesh of the jarana tree in the Brazilian state of Pará. A hundred and fifty feet above, the crown of the jarana shuddered jerkily—spasms strangely like an animal's death throes.

The giant swayed…began to topple. Gathering speed in its fall, it smashed through trees in its path with a roar like a passing train. With a thunderclap it struck the forest floor, so hard the bole splintered.

The tree's impact shook the earth beneath my feet, jarred the pen in my hand. Its true impact reached much farther. With its felling, tiny ecological ripples spread through the environment—like the unforeseen effects of so many of our acts.

*Packed on the Arizona-California border, swarming Lake Havasu boaters typify the pressure put on the environment by a soaring global population of five and a half billion.*

# A PLANET Under Pressure

My jarana was made up largely of carbon; within years the burned or rotted wood would transmute into carbon dioxide, contributing to global warming and intensifying the greenhouse effect. Standing, it had been an ecological asset, capturing and storing carbon dioxide, sweetening the atmosphere with exhalations of oxygen.

The tree's death dealt a wound, minute but measurable, to the surrounding forest community—to the biodiversity of its niche of Amazonia. The nests in its branches, the nectar of its flowers, the carbon that its root hairs fed to fungi, the nutrients it took from the air and pumped into the soil—all of these bore value to the diverse web of life of which it was a part.

The tree's fall ever so slightly changed Amazonia's climate. Each day the roots had drawn up thousands of gallons of groundwater for the leaves to return to the clouds from whence the water had come. The leaves' transpiration and shade had bestowed a coolness. Now the niche was a little drier, a little warmer, and the microclimate in Pará would reflect it.

No one involved in this everyday event had done anything wrong. The chain saw operator needed the job. The landowner needed the wood. Neither intended ill effects for planet Earth. Certainly, neither stood alone in what he had done.

Though Pará is Brazil's most deforested state, I would see much worse in many other places: mountains in the Philippines and northern Pakistan stripped of every tree; slopes in Kenya denuded and eroding; vast tracts of once magnificent forest laid bare in the United States.

Worldwide in scope and profligate in its ill effects, deforestation stands as a symbol of the environmental degradation that so concerns us. Many other stresses vie for our attention: depletion of the ozone layer, with its threat of harmful ultraviolet radiation; loss of reefs and wetlands, so rich in their variety of life-forms; contamination of the air with emissions and the waters with pollutants; and all aggravated by the pressures of a global population rising by a million every four days.

Despite the plethora of ills, a single, transcendent goal unites most environmentalists. The goal is sustainable development: "sustainable" in the sense of protecting the natural environment and, thus, the opportunities of future generations; "development" meaning opportunities for improving the human condition, particularly for the hundreds of millions now living in poverty. Sustainable development provided the theme for the epochal "environmental summit" held in 1992 in Rio de Janeiro.

Are we advancing toward that goal? Not in the opinion of the Washington, D. C.-based World Resources Institute, widely respected for its environmental research. "The world is not now headed toward a sustainable future," stated WRI in a recent volume of its annual compendium, *World Resources*, "but rather toward a variety of potential human and environmental disasters." It decried "the alarming degree to which current patterns of human activity are impoverishing and destabilizing the natural environment and undermining the prospects of future generations."

Nevertheless, the Earth has proved tremendously productive. During the past five decades of exploding population, agricultural productivity rose even faster, until recently. Standards of living, too, rose around the world—not uniformly but on average. But at what cost to sustainability? to future generations?

During a career of science reporting for NATIONAL GEOGRAPHIC magazine, and in travels for this book, I saw my share of altered ecosystems. Usually they had been reshaped either by agriculture or by industry, the two great engines of environmental change. Agriculture has utterly transformed more than a third of the Earth's land surface (excluding Antarctica)—leveled it, plowed it, terraced it, eroded it, drained it, flooded it, grazed it, burned it, even changed its chemistry with fertilizers and other farm chemicals. Industry has altered the atmosphere with its fossil fuel emissions and the water and soil with pollutants. Every individual, of course, also plays a role, from the roadside litterbug to the tanker captain who runs his loaded ship aground to the motorist whose less-than-necessary trip to the store adds car exhausts to greenhouse warming.

The combined effect of these acts casts us, humankind, in two important new roles. Inadvertently, we all have become experimental scientists. Our experiment, wanted by none of us, tests what will happen to a benign, living planet as we change its air, water, soil, and interwoven tapestry of organisms. We play a second role in our experiment: We are its guinea pigs. Every change we impose on the environment we also inflict on ourselves. Fortunately, in swelling numbers we are attempting to minimize and often roll back these impositions.

This rising tide of concern and involvement persists despite—or perhaps because of—a drumfire of negative environmental news that reverberates day after day. These negative reports drown out many of the accomplishments achieved since the environmental reveille sounded with Rachel Carson's *Silent Spring,* in 1962, and the first Earth Day, in 1970. As a result many people—unaware of progress made, of victories won or winnable—succumb to a sense of helplessness, of problems too large to grapple with, and accept as inevitable a steady loss of environmental ground.

## Safeguarding resources

Victories and partial victories, like the problems they address, occur at all levels. What is more localized, and more heartening, than the spread of recycling from town to town, county to county? Each recycler reduces the substantial pollution involved in manufacturing. Each holds down the size of the local landfill and thus curbs the escape of methane, a stealthy greenhouse gas. Each enjoys another prized reward: participation.

At the federal level in the United States, two laws, the Clean Water Act and the Clean Air Act, have brought progress. The aspirations they embody have been matched with enormous effort and financial outlay. Today they and a host of other environmental measures at all levels of government demand expenditures of some 125 billion dollars a year and support an environmental industry that employs nearly a million people.

The Clean Water Act of 1972 and its later amendments represent some of the largest financial commitments of the American people in history. Between 1972 and 1990, the nation spent *(Continued on page 20)*

*Los Angeles is a prime example of the worldwide urban sprawl that paves over*

the land, pollutes the air, and contributes to the threat of global warming.

*Forlorn as tombstones, stumps mark a site being cleared for agriculture in Kenya,*

*where a burgeoning population in need of farmland has depleted the nation's forests.*

*Although ravished land at Brazil's Carajás mine overlies the world's largest deposit of*

*high-quality iron ore, the mine operates with concern for the surrounding rain forest.*

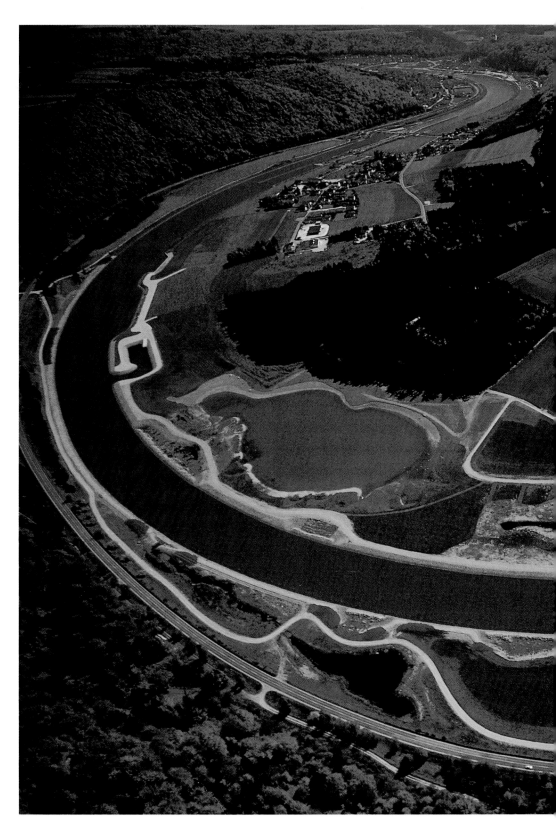

*Designed for minimum environmental damage, the Main-Danube Canal horseshoes*

*through Bavaria's Altmühl Valley. Artificial ponds along the banks nurture wildlife.*

almost 150 billion dollars on sewage treatment facilities alone. Now, instead of rivers so polluted as to be lifeless and even catch fire, waterways by the thousands of miles have been made "swimmable and fishable," along with thousands of acres of lakes. Immense problems remain, particularly with runoff from farms and cities and the constant pressures of development. But the progress is undeniable.

Clean air, despite an annual price tag climbing toward 45 billion dollars, has proved more difficult to attain: three steps forward with successful pollution controls, two steps lost to the new exhaust pipes and smokestacks that we continually add to our present millions. However, experts assert that we are definitely better off than when the Clean Air Act was passed in 1970.

# Successful battles on global issues

A scorecard appears in the World Wildlife Fund's *Atlas of the Environment*. Devastation of the world's whale populations brought on one of the earliest and most hard fought of these battles. In 1946 seafaring nations formed the International Whaling Commission. For more than four decades whaling interests ignored restraints. Not until the 1960s did conservationists make whaling a prominent issue. Today four nations still hunt the leviathans through a loophole allowing catches for "scientific purposes," and Norway has resumed commercial hunting of minkes, but regulations have gone far to thwart commercial whaling.

The WWF scorecard cites a dozen other examples of nations acting in concert to beat back threats to the environment. For instance, concern about the trade in endangered animals and plants provoked the agreement known as CITES, the Convention on International Trade in Endangered Species. The trade continues, but CITES has helped to reduce it. The ugly traffic in ivory, which threatened the extinction of the African elephant in many nations, has "effectively collapsed," reports WWF.

Other international projects and agreements protect vulnerable but as yet relatively undisturbed habitats, such as forests of the Himalayan kingdom of Bhutan and rich wetlands in New Guinea; spare certain forests from wanton logging through the International Tropical Timber Agreement; save the surviving remnants of priceless island forests such as those of hard-hit Madagascar; promote conservation education and national conservation strategies; and control the export of toxic wastes, as in unified actions by nations bordering common seas such as the Mediterranean. "Most significant," notes WWF, is the international control of chemicals that are depleting the ozone layer.

Human life appeared enhanced, not threatened, in the early 1930s when scientists came forth with the chemicals known as chlorofluorocarbons, or CFCs, for refrigerants and other uses. Ammonia, then widely used in refrigerators and air conditioners, was poisonous, and propane, also used, caused explosions. The new CFCs, nontoxic and nonexplosive, were hailed as a major advance.

Use of the miracle chemicals spread worldwide and soared in volume. Then, in the 1970s, American scientists made disturbing calculations:

CFC molecules would rise to the stratosphere and break down Earth's protective ozone layer. Depletion of ozone would permit more of the sun's ultraviolet radiation to reach Earth's surface. This would raise the incidence of skin cancer and cataracts and harm certain plants and animals.

Worried peoples around the world called for controls on CFCs. Continuing research won over more scientists to the peril, including those of the DuPont Company, the major U. S. manufacturer. New impetus emerged in 1985 when British scientists, analyzing American satellite imagery, announced the discovery of an ominous ozone hole—an area of low concentration in the ozone layer—over Antarctica, although there then was no proof that chemical pollutants were to blame.

Seeking to come to grips with the problem, environmental officials from 24 industrial countries gathered in Montreal in 1987. They encountered unprecedented scientific agreement on the danger presented by ozone depletion. They responded in unprecedented international unity. The resulting Montreal Protocol and ensuing London Amendments effectively banned the production of CFCs and other ozone-depleting gases and set a timetable for phasing out their use.

What can one lone, worried person do about the environment? Answers abound in a list of annual winners of the 60-thousand-dollar Goldman Prize, given for individual efforts to protect the Earth. Glimpse a few of these grassroots Nobel Laureates of the environment:

Starting with seedlings grown in her backyard in Nairobi, Wangari Muta Maathai of Kenya launched a women's tree-planting campaign that is acclaimed throughout East Africa as the Green Belt Movement;

Tokyo activist-writer Yoichi Kuroda leads an effort to reform his nation's substantial role in tropical deforestation and the disruption of indigenous forest peoples;

Sam Labudde of the United States made daring, clandestine videos aboard a fishing boat. His pictures led major U. S. tuna canners to stop buying tuna caught in nets that caused the slaughter of dolphins;

Known throughout East Africa as the "Rhino Man," Michael Werikhe of Kenya walked across his nation with a baby rhino on a leash to raise public awareness of the plight of African wildlife;

Peru's Evaristo Nugkuag, a member of the Aguaruna tribe, organized South American Indians—and then their sympathizers in Europe and the United States—to help preserve the Indians' rain forest home.

Could one person, and that person a maverick highly suspect to industry, dethrone a basic axiom of industrial belief? The axiom was that economic growth marches in lockstep with increased use of energy. Amory Lovins, a quiet-spoken Harvard dropout who became Oxford's youngest-ever don, preached the opposite message. Lovins urged energy efficiency as a plausible transition from costly and precarious fossil fuels to renewables such as hydropower, solar, and biomass. Within a few decades, he argued, the United States could enjoy a two-thirds growth in gross national product, unchanged lifestyles, and more jobs—all by painlessly doubling the efficiency of electric motors, tripling that of lights, quadrupling that of

*Concern for Earth's temperature: Dr. Charles David Keeling (opposite) cradles a flask containing a sample of air. Such samples, collected since 1957 from the South Pole to the Arctic, and analyzed by Dr. Keeling and other scientists, have produced graphs that demonstrate vividly the persistent rise of carbon dioxide in Earth's atmosphere. This increase, along with similar measurements of other heat-trapping gases, has led scientists to forecast the greenhouse effect—a warming of Earth's climate. Some warn of heat waves, droughts, crop failures, and famine, accompanied by rising sea levels and coastal flooding. But questions abound. Does the climate show a steady, predictable trend? As NASA's chief scientist for global change, Dr. Ichtiaque Rasool (left) offered a conservative outlook: We do not yet have enough information, he said, to be certain that the planet's climate is consistently warming.*

household appliances, quintupling that of cars, and increasing building efficiency tenfold.

Lovins opened a dialogue with the leviathan U. S. electrical utilities industry, a prodigious consumer of fossil fuels and emitter of pollutants. He and a skilled cadre of number crunchers calculated that there was plenty of wasted electricity out there. To meet rising demand, the utilities merely needed to help their customers become more efficient, and retrieve the conserved electricity for the new customers. More than half the utilities now do this. Today economic growth and energy use defy the old axiom. Since 1973, the economy has grown 47 percent, the use of fossil fuels has increased only 8 percent, and Americans spend 150 billion dollars less a year on energy.

Amory Lovins and his wife, Hunter, direct the Rocky Mountain Institute, a not-for-profit environmental research and educational organization in Snowmass, Colorado. In environmentalese, RMI is known as an NGO—nongovernmental organization. NGOs have become a powerful environmental force.

The *Conservation Directory*, published by the National Wildlife Federation (itself a nongovernmental organization), lists more than 2,000 NGOs for the United States and Canada, many of which work overseas. Broaden

the focus to include state and local groups that support a native species, ecosystem, or neighborhood, and the estimated U. S. total soars to 30,000.

I heard a ringing testimonial to their importance from a leading light of the movement, Dr. George M. Woodwell, whose Woods Hole Research Center conducts pioneering studies of tropical forests and deforestation. "Environmental NGOs are strongest in the United States," said Dr. Woodwell, "where tax laws favor them. They keep pressure on government for environmental protection, much as commerce and industry pressure government in their interests. Two giants in this respect are the Environmental Defense Fund and the Natural Resources Defense Council.

"The NGOs possess enormous expertise," said Dr. Woodwell. "They have more knowledge about the causes and effects of the polluting of air and water than exists in the congressional committees, with their staff turnovers at election times. This is what gives NGOs their ability to influence environmental policy, and to work in developing countries."

The proliferation of U. S. NGOs has proved contagious. "Ten years ago," observed Michael Wright of the WWF, "Colombia had a single environmental group. Now there are close to a thousand. Indonesia has several thousand. In Eastern Europe, the activists who helped overthrow communism and tear down the Berlin Wall are now leading the region's environmental recovery. Africa is behind, but some groups exist to support women and local concerns about water and fuelwood."

Zealous in their role as watchdogs, U. S. NGOs also work with government and multinational players such as the World Bank. In recent years they have been built into government programs, such as the extensive projects of the U. S. Agency for International Development.

USAID funds much of the nation's international environmental outreach, particularly programs for protecting global biodiversity. It conducts its overseas projects almost entirely through NGOs—WWF, the Nature Conservancy, Conservation International, and others involved with hands-on field operations.

At the peak of the NGO pyramid stands the World Resources Institute. Every other year, collaborating with the UN Environment and Development Programmes, WRI updates the eagerly awaited compendium, *World Resources*, designed "to meet the critical need for accessible, accurate information on some of the most pressing issues of our time."

A paramount concern is how to continue feeding the world's soaring population without destroying the environment on which food production depends—how to save Earth's soils and forests when needy people are poised with hoes and chain saws.

Population growth itself stands as another of the great environmental issues. Indeed, for many who worry about the environment, population growth is *the* issue: Relieve the pressure, and we and our comfy blue-green planet could carry on as we always did.

# The figures tell the story

Almost one billion *Homo sapiens* on Earth in 1798 when the Reverend Thomas Robert Malthus intoned: "The power of population is indefinitely greater than the power in the earth to produce subsistence for man." Three and a half billion in 1968, a time of widespread famine when biologist Paul Ehrlich of Stanford University wrote *The Population Bomb*. Four and a half billion in 1982 when the UN Food and Agricultural Organization concluded that even with modern agricultural practices many Third World countries would have difficulty feeding their people by the end of the century. Five and a half billion by the time this book appears, more than six billion by the year 2000.

Looking beyond the near horizon, UN projections see a leveling off in about 2150, when approximately eleven and a half billion of us will share this small and environmentally stressed planet.

In terms of environmental impact, however, population figures tell only part of the story. An equally important factor is affluence. "The birth of a baby in the United States," wrote Dr. Ehrlich and his wife, Dr. Anne Ehrlich, "imposes more than a hundred times the stress on the world's resources and environment as a birth in, say, Bangladesh. Babies from Bangladesh do not grow up to own automobiles and air conditioners or to eat grain-fed beef. Their lifestyles do not require huge quantities of minerals and energy, nor do their activities seriously undermine the life-support capability of the entire planet.

"…Central American forests are destroyed in part for pastureland to make pet food and convenience food in the United States slightly cheaper; in Papua New Guinea forests are destroyed to supply cardboard packaging for Japanese electronic products. Thus a rich person thousands of miles away may cause more tropical forest destruction than a poor person living within the forest itself."

Fortunately, in light of the appetite of affluence, populations in many wealthy countries—although not in the U. S.—are close to stable or declining. On the other hand, the fastest economic growth is occurring in Third World nations—nations with the largest populations. China with 1.2 billion people enjoys an average annual increase in gross national product of about 13 percent. As wealth spreads, so will stress on the environment.

How vulnerable, how delicate, is this Earth? The word *fragile* appears often when we speak of the environment, sometimes almost automatically. And in many ways the environment is extremely fragile. The planet's heat balance, for example. Our releases of greenhouse gases have changed the composition of the atmosphere only microscopically—parts per million. Yet so delicately balanced is the Earth's heating system that almost certainly those gases will soon turn up the thermostat of the entire planet, if they have not already done so.

In other ways, however, the Earth can be viewed as tough indeed. The National Academy of Sciences report, *One Earth, One Future,* observed that "no matter what we humans do, it is unlikely that we could suppress the powerful physical and chemical forces that drive the earth system."

Life itself can be amazingly resilient. I saw this in Kuwait in 1991, when guns of the Gulf War had stilled in Iraq, when the world's greatest oil spill smothered 600 square miles of the Persian Gulf, and when the fires of some 600 dynamited oil wells erupted smoke and soot that many feared would change climate patterns and affect the great African-Asian monsoon.

Probably no known body of water has taken the beating received by the gulf during the war and afterward. Opening oil pipes and blowing up tankers, the Iraqis deliberately spilled as many as twelve million barrels into the already polluted waterway. In places along the coast of Saudi Arabia I saw oil slicks two and three feet thick lapping habitats vital to marine life and birds. These troubled waters are a major Mideast resource: an essential regional fishery, a haven for endemic and migrating bird species, the habitat of rare turtles and the manatee-like dugong.

Far worse pollution fell on the beleaguered gulf from the flaming Kuwait oil wells. At each wellhead, a fine mist of oil rose with the smoke and soot; much fell as an oily drizzle onto the tormented gulf. During the eight months that the wells burned, perhaps as much oil fell on the gulf as had spread upon it in the initial spills.

As firefighters snuffed the last wells, teams of scientists from the United States and other nations investigated the health of the gulf. The investigators feared the worst. Tepid, salty, and shallow, the gulf flushes through the narrow Strait of Hormuz with painful slowness. As expected, the scientists found widespread damage to wildlife—tens of thousands of birds lost, fouled spawning grounds and sea-grass nurseries, beaches paved with slabs of washed-up oil mixed with sand.

They also found offshore reefs and sea-grass communities to be in surprisingly good condition. Despite the avalanche of oil, marine life sampled showed low or no hydrocarbon concentrations in their tissues. "The gulf survived," said Dr. Sylvia Earle, the chief scientist of the National Oceanic and Atmospheric Administration. "But," she added, "it has been forever changed, its chemistry altered. Tolerant creatures will thrive, but others will decline because of the spill and other pollution from the war."

Each blow diminishes the ability of ecosystems to rebound. "Systems are always changing slowly," said William Eichbaum of the WWF. "They can withstand perturbations; they'll continue to roll and change. But each intrusion of our pollutants weakens this resilience—the reproductive capacity, the system's energy flow. Eventually it can't accommodate."

The Kuwait oil fires and their awesome black plume also failed to affect the world's climate. "The fires lacked the energy to project the smoke plume into the stratosphere," said John H. Robinson of NOAA's Gulf Program Office. "The plume from the fires was not detected beyond 1,000 kilometers [621 miles]."

# A scar on the environment

The conflagration had an effect similar to that of millions of gas-guzzling vehicles stalled on a freeway at full throttle. Experts estimate that the wanton burning hurled some 300 million tons of carbon dioxide into the atmosphere. This sad fact was noted halfway around the world, on Hawaii's Mauna Loa. For 35 years, in a mountainside weather observatory run by NOAA, a clever monitoring device has measured the changing carbon dioxide content of the atmosphere. On graph paper this carbon dioxide record appears as an upward-trending curve, somewhat resembling the slope of a ski jump. The rise shows, of course, our ever increasing carbon dioxide emissions and how they steadily accumulate. It is called the Keeling curve, for Dr. Charles David Keeling, the scientist who still doggedly makes the priceless measurements.

Virtually all scientists agree that the Keeling curve accurately shows an exponential rise in atmospheric carbon dioxide. Because carbon dioxide is a powerful greenhouse gas, most scientists (but not all) agree that the curve portends an inevitable increase in global temperatures. Because of this scientific consensus (reminiscent of the consensus on ozone), governments around the world have mobilized against global warming, perhaps the gravest of all long-term threats to the environment.

Scientists from some 60 countries participate in global change research planning through forums such as the International Geosphere-Biosphere Programme. Its task is to "describe...the interactive physical, chemical, and biological processes that regulate the total Earth system, the unique environment it provides for life, the changes that are occurring in this system, and the manner in which they are influenced by human action."

Responding to this mandate, in 1990 an IGBP committee met at the Rockefeller Foundation center in Bellagio, Italy, to chart a course. It recommended dividing the world into 14 ecological regions, each with a regional research network. Special emphasis would be given to the research needs of developing nations. Also, an Inter-American Institute for Global Change Research is taking shape in the Americas, and similar efforts are under way in Europe and Africa and in the Asian-Pacific region.

Substantial leadership for this immense global effort and about half of the total research involved originate with the United States. Eleven U. S. government agencies, coordinated within the Executive Office of the President, devote more than a billion dollars a year to such research. Widely hailed as a landmark in interagency collaboration, the U. S. effort is known as the Global Change Research Program.

For studying the Earth, the program relies heavily on observations from space. During the 1990s and beyond, NASA and counterpart agencies in other nations will launch over 30 missions laden with more than two dozen different sensors for peering down at land, sea, and air over a 15-year period. "We have studied the planets Venus and Mars from orbiting satellites," said Dr. Ichtiaque Rasool, the director of the International Geosphere-Biosphere Programme Data Information System in Paris. "We are also studying Earth."

The NASA program is known as Mission to Planet Earth. The first satellite, launched in 1991, already has returned new information about ozone and the man-made gases that are depleting it.

Monumental as it is, the challenge of understanding the Earth system is merely a means to an end. The ultimate goal is to predict global environmental change. Data from Mission to Planet Earth will be used in computer simulations of how our wastes and pollutants may affect the climate and other aspects of the environment. Scientists call these complex simulations predictive models.

Eventually the computer models will enable scientists to more accurately predict the potential effect of global warming on the climate: the slow rise in temperature here, the lessening of rainfall there, perhaps a rising intensity of storms in the tropics, perhaps a change in the Antarctic ice cap, with its ominous message for global sea levels. When predictive models come of age, they will guide policymakers in how to respond to global climate change, much as the scientific evidence about ozone depletion guided the delegates in Montreal.

In the precarious arena of human governance, the Global Change Research Program is a rare bird: It takes a long view, well beyond the usual political horizon of a few tomorrows. In this, it reflects profound public concern about the environment, and the need to understand the workings of the world we are changing.

*FOLLOWING PAGES: The bright blossoms painting an Iowa meadow are descendants of the first flowering plants that grew millions of years ago. Ralph Waldo Emerson wrote that "Earth laughs in flowers" at prideful human beings who exploit the land for selfish gain.*

I am intruding on a community of the far distant past, here on the murky floor of the Gulf of Mexico. The bacteria surrounding my submersible craft live as did their ancestors at least two billion years ago, converting basic elements of seawater into the rocks that pave the planet. They are illustrating for me the surprising role played by living creatures in creating and regulating the immense Earth ecosystem in which they, we, and rock coexist.

My cramped vessel, the *Johnson SeaLink I,* resembles a tiny helicopter. I sit in the clear plastic-bubble cockpit with pilot Don Liberatore, on his 981st descent to the depths.

*"Well may we affirm that every part of the world is habitable!" wrote naturalist Charles Darwin. In Nevada, a hot spring attests to his words as home to tenacious bacteria.*

We had launched from the research vessel *Seward Johnson*, on charter by Louisiana State University to explore the petroleum-rich basin that nurtures the rare community frozen in *SeaLink*'s headlights.

I eye a small crater 15 feet in front of us. B-u-r-p! It erupts with a burst of bubbles. "Methane—natural gas," explains Dr. Harry Roberts of LSU, the project organizer, now crammed in the tapering stern of our craft. "It's being manufactured by bacteria living in the bottom sediments."

Around the bubbling crater spreads a fuzzy white mat nearly the size of a basketball court. "*Beggiatoa* bacteria—among the largest known," says Dr. Roberts. "Primitive bacteria inhabited the planet before the evolution of photosynthesis. Instead of harnessing sunlight, they generate energy chemically, from hydrogen and sulfur. They built much of this environment down here.

"See that rock?" he asks. How can I miss it—a towering, angular boulder that I hope our pilot will not ram. "That's calcium carbonate, good old limestone, made by the chemical reactions of these and other Gulf floor bacteria. You're seeing rock being born from living creatures."

Earth and life: It is an intimate partnership, unique in the solar system. Only recently has it been appreciated. In the past we viewed the physical, inanimate Earth as a rigid matrix that imposed its conditions on life. Plants and animals passively adapted.

Today we recognize that living organisms vastly influence the Earth they inhabit. Not only do they make rock, as I saw on the floor of the Gulf of Mexico. They profoundly affect ocean chemistry. They helped create the present atmosphere. Thus they affect even the climate.

Today all of these parts are seen as players in a vast and intricate web of interactions known collectively as the Earth system. Partly in response to environmental concerns, a new discipline has arisen known as Earth system science. It is based on the premise that we must understand the entire, interworking system if we are to understand our impacts on it. This understanding must embrace Earth's violent beginnings, when rock, water, and the stuff of life coalesced in space to form our planet.

Scientists seeking to reconstruct Earth's origins face an immediate problem: The violence of these early events, and subsequent tectonic activity, erased most of their remains. Fortunately, fragmentary records exist beyond the planet, in sources unaffected by that early turbulence. The record hides encrypted in the ancient rock brought to Earth by meteorites, and in rocks brought home by astronauts who prowled the moon.

Some of the most dramatic clues were borne to Earth by Australia's famous Murchison meteorite and by the Allende meteorite that fell spectacularly on northern Mexico in 1969. In the Murchison meteorite, organic material and volatile gases trapped inside diamond dust told scientists that the meteorite had escaped the violent heating that took place during the formation of the solar system; thus it harbored materials predating that event. The Allende meteorite, shattering the predawn darkness over Chihuahua with sonic booms and a midair explosion that broke it into thousands of fragments, also contained elements in forms not found today on Earth.

These and other meteorites give scientists unique information about the types and behavior of exploded stars whose gas and debris made up the cloud that evolved into the solar system—a glimpse of the "stellar factory," in the words of Professor Gerald J. Wasserburg of the California Institute of Technology.

About 4.6 billion years ago, scientists theorize, this rotating cloud of stellar gas and debris probably was rocked by the shock wave of a star exploding nearby.

Nudged by the shock wave and tugged by gravity, the cloud compressed, forcing solid particles together in clumps—the process of accretion. Most matter gravitated to form the future sun. Some matter accreted into outlying aggregations to give birth to the planets. In its slow rotation, the cloud of debris flattened into the disk of today's solar system.

The early sun did not shine. Instead it glared coldly through a rain of impacting debris. Steadily it grew. Finally its own gravity collapsed it inward. Pressure heated its core and ignited its nuclear furnace, in which hydrogen atoms fused into helium and released vast heat. For the first time, sunlight bathed the still growing Earth.

There, chaos reigned. Impacting space debris splashed into the largely molten planetoid. The metallic iron in these bodies immediately sank to form the planet's core, initiating Earth's magnetic field even as the planet grew. Volcanoes far more numerous than today's spewed geysers of molten glass.Massive jets of steam erupted from the depths and unfurled an atmosphere too hot for condensation and rain.

In the most massive cataclysm of all, a body perhaps as large as Mars smashed into Earth and blasted into space a massive chunk of the still partly liquid mantle. The moon was born.

Despite these upheavals, no other planet in the nascent solar system offered conditions so favorable for life.

As the third planet out from the sun, Earth basked in abundant solar energy while avoiding the fate of the nearer planets: Venus, where the sun's heat prevents water vapor from condensing into oceans, and closest-orbiting Mercury, where the intense solar radiation blasted its atmosphere into space.

# The water of life

Earth's size allowed it to retain the internal heat necessary to later drive plate tectonics, a process that recycles carbon dioxide and  perhaps helps to stabilize the climate. Best of all, Earth—and probably only Earth—offered an environment bathed in liquid water, the medium essential to all known life. Its source was the early, thunderous volcanoes and ice brought to Earth by incoming comets, meteorites, and asteroids, which vaporized on impact. When the Earth cooled sufficiently, this moisture condensed, fell as rain, and

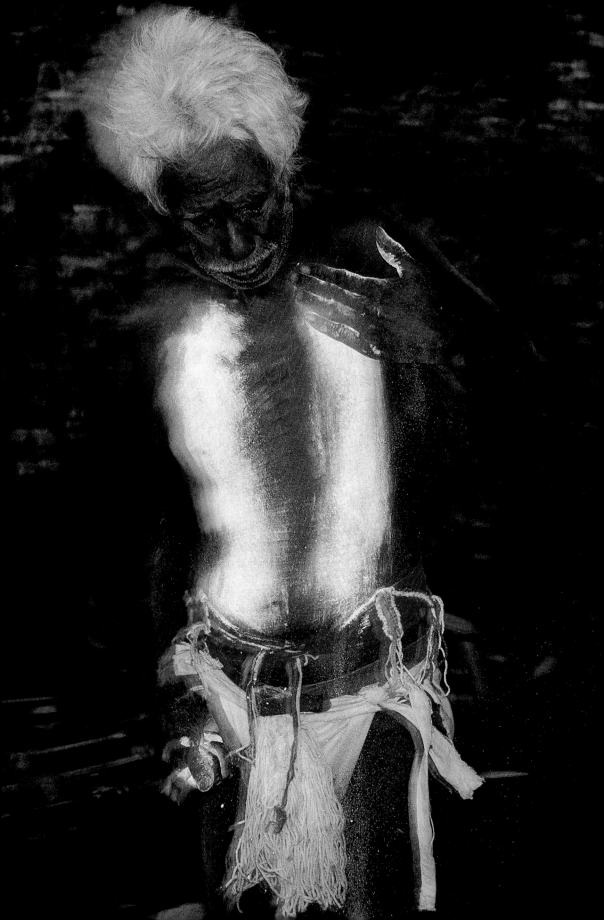

gradually filled lakes and oceans—the future wombs of living organisms.

Volcanoes supplied other ingredients of life. They belched out nitrogen, the key to proteins and nucleic acids. They exhaled carbon dioxide, a source of indispensable carbon. Only carbon atoms offered the architecture for fashioning the long-chain molecules required to sustain living organisms.

With the stage thus set, life emerged—some say miraculously, some say inevitably. In a Harvard office where shelves sagged with fossil-bearing rocks, Dr. Andrew Knoll described the stage on which the emergence took place.

"The early atmosphere probably consisted of water vapor, nitrogen, carbon dioxide, a little hydrogen, and perhaps a pinch of methane," he said. "According to our best calculations of a 'life-origin' formula, these were the ingredients that favored life's creation."

How far back did it occur? "We find fossils of early life-forms in South Africa and Australia dating back 3.5 billion years—as far back as we can find sedimentary rock to preserve them," said Dr. Knoll. "Rocks found in Isua, Greenland, hint that life traces back at least 3.8 billion years, but the rock has been metamorphosed by heat and pressure and doesn't present a clearly legible record.

"Either way, the dates are impressive when you recall that the Earth was under intense bombardment by meteorites until 3.9 billion years ago. Tectonic activity has erased evidence of that bombardment, but craters preserved on the surface of the moon show that some of the impacts would have been life-terminating for Earth organisms.

"Even during the course of the bombardment, however," Dr. Knoll pointed out, "there could have been repeated experiments with life, experiments that failed. Although Earth's record is gone, we someday could find evidence on Mars, where conditions favorable to life paralleled those on Earth and have not been erased by tectonism."

That first cellular life-form was a bacterium, a microscopic, single-cell, self-maintaining sac of proteins possessing a unique capability: that of self-replication. All of its disparate descendants across four and a half billion years would share the spiraled genetic material introduced in that first bacterium—the universal language of heredity we know as DNA and RNA.

## Faint traces in the rocks

While life was forming, the planet was steadily cooling, radiating into space the heat accumulated during the bombardments of accretion. Simultaneously, another mighty heat source was *(Continued on page 40)*

*An Australian Aborigine smears himself with pigments for a corroboree—songs and dances that recall the Dreamtime, when ancient spirits shaped Earth's features.*

*FOLLOWING PAGES: Rising head and shoulders from the sea, an Antarctic iceberg dwarfs a research vessel. Scientists theorize that volcanic ash formed the dark layers.*

Earth's oldest known communities of life, stromatolites cluster in the warm, shallow waters of the Caribbean, where a diver measures their growth. Survivors from the age of bacteria, these colonizing organisms have lived on the planet virtually unchanged for some 3.5 billion years, using energy from the sun to manufacture food and oxygen. Stromatolites form when sediment covers mats of bacteria. The bacteria cement the sediment together, then grow over it. Time gave rise to land plants, such as ferns (opposite, right). Some land plants, such as the oxygen-beaded Elodea (opposite, left), have returned to live in water.

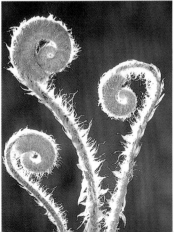

making itself felt, this one internal. Three of Earth's elements—uranium, thorium, and potassium—were radioactive. Permeating the flesh of the youthful planet, they decayed and released heat. This heat would keep Earth's core molten for the billions of years to follow, and set the stage for plate tectonics, in which the continents and sea floors move grandly about Earth atop the semimolten mantle.

Heady geology. But bacteria were keeping pace. For two billion years they would rule the Earth, boldly reshaping their boundless frontier. In their book, *Microcosmos: Four Billion Years of Evolution from Our Microbial Ancestors,* Dorion Sagan and University of Massachusetts professor Lynn Margulis wrote: "With sleep unknown to them they grew, consumed energy and organic chemicals, and divided incessantly. Their colonies and fibers interconnected and covered the sterile globe in a spotty film. The dimensions of this film have expanded into a patina of life, or biosphere, the place where life exists....The Age of Bacteria transformed the earth from a cratered moonlike terrain of volcanic glassy rocks into the fertile planet in which we make our home."

The first act in this transformation was the greatest. I learned of it in the laboratory of Dr. Clinton Fuller, also at the University of Massachusetts. "This piece of rock from Australia," he said, thrusting a fist-size chunk in my direction, "was part of a fossilized stromatolite, an ancient bacterial colony. We have dated it at 3.5 billion years. The fossil bacteria in such rocks appear identical to bacteria alive today. The living species performs photosynthesis, the converting of sunlight and carbon dioxide into useful energy. There's every reason to believe that the early bacteria also performed photosynthesis.

"This indicates that bacteria developed photosynthesis soon after they evolved, when the planet still was hot and gassy. Keep in mind that photosynthesis is the single most important innovation in evolution. Virtually all life depends either on the production of carbohydrates by photosynthesis or on eating the animals that feed on those carbohydrates."

Without photosynthesis, the planet's only inhabitants might be microbes surviving by chemosynthesis, such as organisms that live at high temperatures in hot springs environments.

As if bacteria still held a patent for their invention, photosynthesis has never been replicated in the laboratory. At Washington University in St. Louis, ingenious research is revealing the astonishing efficiency of that early innovation.

Professors Chris Kirmaier and Dewey Holten explained to me that the energy for photosynthesis is captured when a photon—a particle of light—strikes the bacteria's reaction chamber. Miraculously, every photon that enters the chamber scores a bull's-eye, boosting an electron across a membrane, thus the light-capturing efficiency in the ancient process of photosynthesis is 100 percent.

Early bacteria brought forth two more inventions fundamental to shaping the Earth system.

For complex life to evolve, it had to harness the element nitrogen, essential for making proteins and nucleic acids. Nitrogen is abundant in the air, but its extraction requires vast energy, such as that contained in lightning bolts.

Bacteria mastered the chemistry of nitrogen fixing more than three billion years ago. On them all life has depended; no other creatures have acquired this ability except by the symbiotic incorporation of bacteria. Today nitrogen availability still is one of the limiting factors of life's abundance in the environment.

The other great invention involved oxygen. Early in the age of bacteria, the atmosphere and oceans were virtually oxygen free, and the first photosynthetic bacteria obtained their hydrogen from gases such as hydrogen sulfide.

Then, about three billion years ago, bacteria hungering for hydrogen invented a new kind of photosynthesis that used the sun's energy to split water molecules—to separate hydrogen from oxygen.

The bacteria used the hydrogen for making carbohydrates, the stuff of today's plants and animals and, indirectly, fossil fuels. They had no use for the oxygen, and they cast it off as a waste product, to bubble up from the mud and slime. Now the slow-burn process of oxidation could take place. As fast as oxygen was released by the bacteria, it was consumed by chemical reactions with gases, dissolved metals, and rocks. Not until about two billion years ago was oxygen produced fast enough to accumulate in the atmosphere.

Some wafted up to the stratosphere, where it united with other oxygen to produce ozone. These robust molecules could absorb the energy of deadly ultraviolet radiation. Gradually, enough stratospheric ozone accumulated to stop virtually all lethal ultraviolet from reaching Earth's surface. This umbrella, some experts believe, permitted organisms to venture out of the protective waters and claim a place in the sun.

Exposure to the aggressive oxygen was lethal to bacteria that had lived without it—and this meant most of them. The spread of the gas, scientists believe, caused the first of Earth's great extinctions. The oxygen holocaust, in the words of Dorion Sagan and Lynn Margulis, "was by far the greatest pollution crisis the earth has ever endured."

# Life remodels the Earth

Organisms that adapted to oxygen, however, enjoyed an evolutionary leap. They were the respirers, the breathers. By taking in oxygen for its controlled combustion with body sugars, as occurs in our blood, the breathers generated enormous energy. With oxygen in the air, the world was ready for more than microbes.

And the higher life-forms came, in slow but gathering procession. Catastrophic extinctions would punctuate this grand pageant of evolution. But always life would rebound and advance in the dynamic arena of the Earth system.

The earliest animals flourish in the seas about 580 million years ago, just before the beginning of the Cambrian period. Mud-living

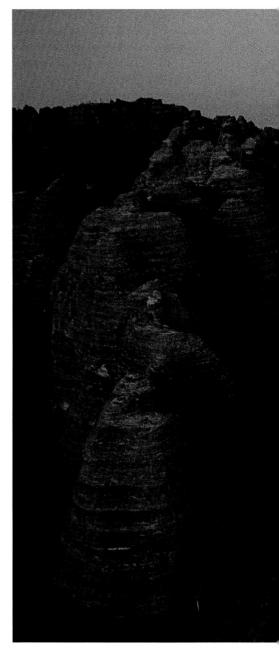

Remnants of a world long gone
linger in Earth's tantalizing fossil
record. In Australia's Bungle
Bungle Range, seas laid down the
370-million-year-old sandstone
layers that erosion has carved into
beehive shapes. In shallow seabeds
swam nautilus-like ammonites—
a group that died out 65 million
years ago. Tree resin entombed an
ancient insect in amber. A dagger-
toothed, 12-foot-long fish ranged
the inland sea of North America
85 million years ago.

trilobites and spongelike reef builders soon come to reign in this time of biological ferment. They eventually decline in importance as other groups diversify.

In the Ordovician period, sea-living nautiloids, corals, and sea lilies rise to dominate. Again a massive die-off strikes, about 463 million years ago. It coincides with a time when plate tectonics carries the supercontinent Gondwana to the South Pole, triggering severe glaciation.

Reef builders flourish anew in the Devonian period, and large fishes have evolved; the earliest woody plants sprout in Devonian soils. Most fishes and 70 percent of other marine animals become extinct 370 million years ago, perhaps because of the impact of a large asteroid or meteorite, or because shallow marine habitats became flooded with oxygen-shy water from the depths.

Insects swarm in the Permian period, a time when landmasses merge in the supercontinent Pangaea. At water's edge prowl large amphibians and rudimentary reptiles. About 250 million years ago, they fall to the greatest extinction ever, claiming 96 percent of all species. The great dying may occur in pulses spread over eight million years.

Further extinctions of uncertain origin wrack the Triassic and Jurassic periods, when evolution is honing bigger and better dinosaurs. The great reptiles have their heyday in the Cretaceous period. Perhaps a hundred species roam, some warm-blooded, some wearing feathers or fur.

About 65 million years ago, a mighty cataclysm, possibly an asteroid impact or a reduction in the level of atmospheric oxygen, snuffs out the great reptiles, and makes way for the mammalian ancestors of *Homo sapiens.*

Today a colliding of continents controls much of the climate of the Earth system, including the great Asian-African monsoon, the pulse of life for two billion of the world's people. About 40 million years ago the plate carrying India, moving north across the Indian Ocean, rammed into the belly of the giant Eurasian plate. The collision began the uplift of the Himalaya and the lofty Tibetan Plateau. Though not as famous as the Himalaya, the plateau is awesome. A third as large as the United States, it contains more than 90 percent of the Earth's surface that is at least 13,000 feet above sea level.

Each summer the air above the plateau heats and rises. The rising air mass serves as a mighty exhaust piston, pulling in moisture-laden air from the Indian Ocean. The moist air brings the life-sustaining monsoon rains to South Asia. Each winter the mammoth engine reverses its stroke, and moist air brings rain to thirsty areas of northern Africa.

Many scientists believe the Tibetan Plateau affects the Earth system in three other ways:

First, the uplift of the plateau and the nearly simultaneous rising of the Colorado Plateau in the western United States changed global wind patterns. These two events cooled the planet and thus helped to bring on the great Ice Age of the past two and a half million years.

Second, they think that winds from the plateau stir immense dust storms in the Sahara and the deserts of Asia, and that these play an important role in determining climate.

Third, the torrential monsoon rains falling on the Himalaya pick up large amounts of atmospheric carbon dioxide, which reacts with eroding rock and flushes to sea to form limestone—thus removing the carbon dioxide as a greenhouse gas and helping cool the Earth.

Scientists studying the Ice Age found that the great ice sheets advanced and retreated in pulses that show an almost clocklike rhythm. For the scientists the rhythm posed no mystery. It fits a pattern of Earth-system cycles known as the Milankovitch effect.

Astronomers have long known that Earth's orbital movements vary cyclically over time. In the 1920s, the Yugoslavian astronomer Milutin Milankovitch calculated these cycles: Every 96,000 years the Earth's orbit around the sun varies its elliptical shape; every 41,000 years the tilt of Earth's axis changes from 21.8° to 24.4°; and about every 21,000 years the axis completes a wobble of about a degree.

The orbital changes ever so slightly affect the angle at which sunlight strikes the atmosphere. Though small, these variations profoundly affect how much heat reaches Earth's surface. Their impact increases when two or three occur simultaneously. In effect, the cycles are the pacemakers of the ice ages. During the 2.5 million years of the last ice age, the Milankovitch pacemaker has triggered a score of glacial onslaughts. The last probably was the most severe.

# A frozen world

Flying across North America recently, I looked down on a continent covered by snow from coast to coast. It was not difficult, at 35,000 feet above the frozen upper Midwest, to imagine that this was how the top of the ice sheet appeared 18,000 years ago, at the peak of the last great glacial advance. Beyond the southern horizon, I visualized woolly mammoths browsing trees toppled by the towering ice wall.

This last glacial episode, probably typical of most, was a relentless engine of environmental change. About 100,000 years ago, heavy snows — more than can melt in the summers—fall over northern and eastern Canada. Ice begins to accumulate, one year's on top of the last. Centered over present Hudson Bay and highlands to the east, the ice relentlessly builds: a hundred feet high, a thousand feet high. Five thousand feet. Ten thousand.

Like stiff molasses poured on a pancake, the ice spreads outward under its own weight; it creeps unstoppably southward. The base of the glacier picks up soil, stones, and boulders—trillions of tons of abrasive grit; now the slab is a planetary rasp, grinding down highlands, filling valleys. Its stupendous weight bends down the rock of the Canadian Shield a thousand feet, forming the depression of Hudson Bay.

By 18,000 years ago, the glacial maximum, ice more than two miles thick crushes the northland. The great white carapace covers much of Canada; lobes of ice a mile thick engulf the area of the northern

United States from the Dakotas to Ohio to northern New Jersey and southern New England. The great continental ice sheets in North America and Eurasia hold so much of the world's water that they deplete the oceans, dropping worldwide sea levels by 360 feet or more. The markedly lower levels reduce the area of the oceans and seas and significantly increase the land area, producing very different continent and island configurations and creating land bridges in some areas.

At last temperatures rise, and irregularly the ice retreats. It leaves in its wake a land transformed: a Midwest spangled with lakes and tattooed with drumlins, eskers, and kettles; a Northeast ramped with monadnocks and strewn with smoothed stones for future fences; an Atlantic coast hemmed with the great terminal moraines we know as Long Island and Cape Cod; an abundance of precious, glacier-given groundwater.

Following each retreat of the ice sheets, the Northern Hemisphere enjoyed warm spells known as interglacials. These were brief, as short as 10,000 years—the time that has elapsed since the last glacial retreat. The obvious question: Are we basking in a temporary interglacial that perhaps is nearing its end? Earth scientists are still trying to resolve this.

Paralleling the Ice Age, a biological event was unfolding that would rival the glaciers in shaping the future Earth system: the emergence of human beings. Armed with a thumb, a brain, and an ever growing arsenal of tools, including fire, humankind is a species uniquely equipped to alter its environment. The history of environmental degradation goes back far, despite popular generalizations that earlier peoples universally enjoyed a protective oneness with nature.

Indeed, these early marks on the environment are as far-flung as are the areas of human occupation. About 40,000 years ago—and perhaps much earlier—when Ice Age oceans ebbed, fire-using Aborigines crossed from Indonesia into Australia; quickly Australian vegetation changed, soon to be dominated by the fire-tolerant eucalyptus tree.

Destruction of the environment of the Mediterranean littoral dates to the grazing of sheep about 7,000 years ago; more than 2,000 years ago the Greek philosopher Plato saw about him "the mere skeleton of the land."

The removal of 90 percent of Britain's forests proceeded remorselessly over a span of 3,000 to 4,000 years.

Not even paradise escaped. Archaeological exploration reveals that by 1,600 years ago South Sea islanders were altering the ecosystem of Mangaia Island by deforestation, erosion, extinction of native birds, and a growing dependence on agriculture.

*A menagerie of the missing surrounds a curator at the Tring Zoological Museum in England. Among the extinct species: a skeletal giant ground sloth, the zebra-like quagga, the striped Tasmanian wolf, and the dodo. Although global catastrophes have killed off millions of species, human activity now is the prime agent of extinctions.*

In the New World, deforestation probably contributed to the abandonment of the remarkable Chacoan settlements of the Anasazi Indians of the Southwest. Nearly a thousand years ago the industrious Anasazi cut timbers by the tens of thousands to support the roofs of their great pueblos in Chaco Canyon and outlying communities. With neither the wheel nor beast of burden, they reached as far as 75 miles for logs before the collapse. Fuelwood would have been as scarce—a problem familiar today in many nations.

Today, of course, the human role has exploded; its impact extends beyond localized disturbances to the planetary—to human-induced perturbations on a scale of the Milankovitch effect and the uplift of the Tibetan Plateau. To key player in the Earth system.

The significance of this new role found blunt expression in a declaration of NASA's Earth System Sciences Committee:

"We, the peoples of the world, face a new responsibility for our global future. Through our economic and technological activity, we are now contributing to significant global changes of the Earth within the span of a few human generations. We have become part of the Earth System and one of the forces for Earth change."

# Earth's system at work

Recent studies of Earth's past and its daily workings have established the system's broad outlines. In the planet's interior, powered by the heat of radioactive decay, the semimolten mantle drives giant crustal plates that bear the continents, build mountains, and plunge back into the mantle to recycle minerals.

Weathering erodes mountains almost as fast as they rise, and flushes their minerals down to become sediments that later will be pushed up again as mountains. Even though geologic cycles unfold across eons, other geological processes confront us daily—as volcanic eruptions, earthquakes, dust storms, and tsunamis.

This churning rind of rock and sediment interacts with the system's other players, all driven by solar energy. These are the atmosphere, oceans, ice areas, and biosphere.

The atmosphere. Composed of 78 percent nitrogen and 21 percent oxygen, the atmosphere holds other gases whose relatively small quantities belie their vast importance: the water vapor of rain, the carbon dioxide of plant production, the ozone of our radiation shield. The atmosphere acts as a benign greenhouse, trapping the day's heat against the frigidity of night. The trapped heat drives Earth's weather machine—the evaporation and condensation of rain, the temperature differences that cause the winds. Nine newly discovered rivers of water vapor, each more than 400 miles wide and carrying as much water as the Amazon, transfer heat and moisture from the tropics toward the Poles.

The oceans. Covering 70 percent of the surface and locking up 97 percent of the planet's water, the oceans are vast reservoirs of heat and dissolved minerals. Prevailing winds drive ocean currents such as the Gulf Stream, controlling the temperatures of much of the world. Ocean currents in turn serve as a mighty flywheel that drives the climate. The ocean's dissolved minerals and other nutrients support zooplankton and phytoplankton, the base of the oceanic food chain. Salt and other particles escape into the atmosphere to form the nuclei of raindrops.

The ice regions. The polar regions are increasingly recognized as major shapers of the climate; 77 percent of all fresh water is locked in ice, primarily in Antarctica and Greenland. The polar ice sheets and sea ice affect the salinity and temperature of polar ocean water, setting in motion vast subsurface currents that affect the global distribution of heat and nutrients.

The biosphere. Consisting of the living organisms of land, sea, and air, the biosphere interacts with every other Earth subsystem. Geologically it lays down not only corals and limestone but also vast deposits of coal and petroleum. It affects the climate in myriad ways, and thus the oceans, land cover, and atmosphere. Most important, through the processes of respiration and decay it influences the carbon cycle, the flow of that structural element of life through the land, sea, and air.

L ike the organisms within it, the entire Earth breathes, in two different cadences, one daily and one seasonal. One of these cadences was discovered by Dr. Charles David Keeling, whose measurements of atmospheric carbon dioxide read like a stethoscope on the lungs of the world.

Dr. Keeling recalled that heady early work: "Back in the '50s when I first began measuring, I went to the Big Sur area of California. In the morning before sunrise I counted 380 parts per million of carbon dioxide. That same afternoon I got 315 parts. I realized that I was seeing the forest's daily breathing—its release of carbon dioxide at night when the plants are not photosynthesizing, its inhalations during the sunlight hours when they are photosynthesizing.

"After I placed a carbon dioxide analyzer on Mauna Loa in Hawaii, I encountered a puzzling irregularity. The reading for atmospheric carbon dioxide changed month by month. Soon I saw a pattern. The line dipped in the spring and summer, when daylight hours were longest in the Northern Hemisphere, and rose during winter when darkness was greater. This reflected the fact that during the months of long daylight the plants of the entire hemisphere were inhaling carbon dioxide for photosynthesis. I had measured an *annual* cycle of breathing on a planetary scale."

To keep this breathing cycle strong and steady—that is the goal of Earth system science and environmental sustainability.

*FOLLOWING PAGES: Visitors watch a fiery display on the flanks of Hawaii's Kilauea, the world's most active volcano. Volcanoes began building the island chain some 70 million years ago. This eruption began in 1983, and has added 470 acres to the island's area.*

# The AIR We Breathe

Charles David Keeling, chronicler of the carbon dioxide build-up, adjusted his steel-rim reading glasses and leaned across his work-piled desk at the Scripps Oceanographic Institution. The unpretentious chemist gave the look of a man who wished to be heard. I listened.

"The greenhouse process is here," he said, referring to the global warming effect of the carbon dioxide increase he has so accurately measured. "When I began analyzing in 1958, the $CO_2$ level in the atmosphere was 315 parts per million. Now it's 355 parts per million.

"The effect of the $CO_2$ increase is as if we placed a

*Steam, smoke, and clouds mingle to make a murky day near Vancouver, Canada. Industry today faces a formidable challenge: to produce goods efficiently—and cleanly.*

two-watt bulb on every square yard of the Earth's surface and turned them all on." I recalled that two watts was the size of the larger bulbs I'd placed on our family Christmas tree. With Earth's surface encompassing more than 500 trillion square yards, Dr. Keeling was talking major wattage.

Dr. Keeling and, in fact, most scientists when they are speaking for the record draw up short of asserting that global warming is already a measurable phenomenon. But almost all agree that it *will* happen, if it hasn't already. After all, the increase in carbon dioxide and other human-induced greenhouse gases is real, the heat-trapping quality of the gases is real, and the 1980s was the warmest decade in weather records.

Few question the leading source of the increasing $CO_2$. It is the massive burning of fossil fuels that has powered the great engine of industrialization. Until the industrial era, nature for hundreds of millions of years had systematically removed carbon from the air and locked it away underground as coal, oil, and natural gas. By sequestering this carbon in the ground, the natural system maintained a fairly even level of carbon dioxide in the atmosphere—one of numerous mysterious, self-regulating mechanisms that help stabilize the great Earth organism.

Then the boilers, furnaces, and internal combustion engines that power industry and transportation began gorging on the carbon of unearthed fossil fuels. Today the energy industry—the world's largest— extracts the stored carbon in amounts that must be hollowing out the planet: five billion tons of coal a year, three billion tons of oil, 73 trillion cubic feet of natural gas. As they go up in smoke, the fuels pump an awesome *six billion tons* of invisible carbon a year into the atmosphere. This accounts for much of the $CO_2$ increase that Charles David Keeling records on his atmospheric analyzer—the upswing of the Keeling curve.

With five-plus billion of us inhabiting the Earth, this means each of us sends up on average about a ton of carbon a year. But averages don't apply in a world of haves and have-nots. In the developed countries, an individual burns about four times as much fossil fuel as a counterpart in a developing country. And the United States burns by far the most of any nation. Where an average Chinese accounts for about half a ton of carbon a year, for the individual in the United States the average is five tons.

Not all the blame for $CO_2$ falls on fossil fuels. The role of deforestation was identified in 1977, in a paper by Dr. George M. Woodwell of the Woods Hole Research Center and his colleague Richard A. Houghton. A standing tree, the writers said, is a storehouse of carbon, just as are underground coal, oil, and natural gas. When we cut trees down and burn them to make way for pasture or farmland, we release that carbon for global warming. The scientists reasoned that if forests are falling faster than they are growing, then very likely deforestation is adding to the greenhouse effect.

The link spurred closer monitoring of deforestation by satellite. The findings supplied a crucial element of the global carbon dioxide picture. "The satellite imagery," said Dr. David Skole of the University of New Hampshire, "tells us that the burning accompanying deforestation adds about a billion tons of carbon a year to the atmosphere."

A weighty carbon mystery still plagues scientists. Each year we spew a billion tons into the air that cannot be accounted for. The mystery brings on acute discomfort among those concerned about global climate change. I received a quick review from Dr. Edward S. Sarachik, a University of Washington oceanographer who plays a key role in the international effort to understand human influences on our climate.

"We're reasonably sure that six billion tons of carbon are released into the atmosphere each year by the burning of fossil fuels," said Dr. Sarachik. "Deforestation adds another billion tons—that's seven.

"So we ask ourselves, 'Where is it all going?', and we can only account for six billion of those seven billion tons. Three billion tons remain in the atmosphere—the amount recorded as the Keeling curve. The oceans probably absorb one or two billion tons. Another billion seem to be taken up by forests and soils. That leaves at least a billion tons unaccounted for—it disappears into a sink we can't identify.

"Why does this bother us? We worry that the sink might be unstable—sensitive to climate change. The onset of global warming could cause the sink to stop absorbing carbon dioxide. Then that billion tons could remain in the atmosphere and intensify the greenhouse effect."

# Panes in the chemical greenhouse

Three other gases contribute to the chemical greenhouse we humans are building around the planet: nitrous oxide, chlorofluorocarbons, or CFCs—the same CFCs that deplete the ozone layer—and methane. Together the three trap as much heat as do our emissions of $CO_2$.

The world knew nitrous oxide as laughing gas when dentists used it as an anesthetic before the advent of Novocain. Today it earns attention as a greenhouse gas because of each molecule's long and destructive life in the atmosphere—about 200 years. A principal source is believed to be the breakdown of nitrogen fertilizers, particularly in warm soils of the tropics where agriculture is expanding the fastest; other sources are slash-and-burn agriculture and the emissions of fossil fuels and rayon manufacturing. Precision applications of fertilizers are a partial cure for nitrous oxide emissions and other environmental problems caused by nitrates. The gas constitutes about 5 percent of the human addition to the greenhouse effect.

CFCs, already convicted of ozone destruction, are also major villains of global warming. The gases survive in the atmosphere as long as 400 years and trap heat thousands of times more effectively than $CO_2$. Thus their effects will linger long after their scheduled phaseout by the year 2000. CFCs contribute some 20 percent of total human-induced warming.

Environmentalists cock a wary eye at methane. The atmospheric concentration of this ubiquitous gas has doubled in the past century and a half, and has been increasing at a rate as high as one percent a year—double that of $CO_2$. Most is generated by bacteria breaking down organic matter in the absence of oxygen—in landfills; in the stomachs of cows, which belch it out in clouds; and in wetlands and flooded rice fields, where plant stems serve as little chimneys for the gas's escape. Methane also rises from the burning of fields and forests, and the extraction, delivery, and processing

of fossil fuels. Enormous amounts lie trapped in the vast frozen wetlands of northern tundra, and could be released by global warming.

"Methane also may be our most manageable greenhouse gas," I heard from Dr. Robert C. Harriss of the University of New Hampshire. "If we reduce releases by 15 percent, we can stabilize methane concentrations in the atmosphere. The best opportunities for methane mitigation are in cities, where much of the methane related to human activities is produced."

An activist as well as an academic, Dr. Harriss sallies forth into the cities to measure their methane metabolism. "We equipped a van with a laser sensor that detects methane. Traveling at roadway speeds, we execute a series of traverses across a city, recording methane emissions as we go. We end up with a map of the city's methane concentrations. The hot spots are usually landfills, wastewater treatment plants, and natural-gas distribution points. Our map gives a city the information it needs to enact an abatement program. It can tap the methane at the landfill and water treatment plant, and plug the leaks in its gas system. Methane control is doable."

## The premiere greenhouse gas

Can we control carbon dioxide? It's happening, and nowhere more energetically than in California. Lead by the skillful negotiating of environmentalists and a sympathetic state commission, the four largest utilities broke with the timeworn policy of promoting electricity sales and embraced a new credo of energy efficiency and its happy by-product— massive reductions of $CO_2$.

"The energy savings of the California utilities during the next decade," said Amory Lovins of the Rocky Mountain Institute, chief architect of the new approach, "will mean a $CO_2$ reduction of about a billion tons." The utilities' conversion to the new faith of energy efficiency is seen as a crucial turning point in the long march toward the sustainability of life on planet Earth. Why did they do it?

"As long as the utilities profited only by *selling* electricity," explained Ralph Cavanagh of the Natural Resources Defense Council, who served as chief catalyst in the negotiations, "they would promote energy use. We had to break that linkage, and forge a new linkage between utility profits and energy *efficiency*."

In 1990, through groundwork laid by Mr. Cavanagh, the regulators joined with environmentalists, consumer groups, and the utilities and agreed to a new formula. The more energy a utility induced a customer to save, the more money the utility made. The agreement, known as "the collaborative," scored a second victory for the environment. With electrical demand reduced, the utility could absorb *(Continued on page 64)*

*Marble transformed into a coating of crumbly gypsum by the chemical action of sulfurous smog covers a monument honoring King Victor Emmanuel II in a Roman square.*

*FOLLOWING PAGES: Hong Kong's bright lights display a dark side, too: Each year the world's electric power companies burn millions of tons of polluting fossil fuels.*

*Onshore or offshore, the extraction of fossil fuels goes on, feeding the world's appetite for energy. In California's San Joaquin Valley (opposite), a roustabout checks an oil rig. On a North Sea drilling platform, excess gas flares off during a test of a new field. In Wyoming, a huge dragline dwarfs workers at the Black Thunder Mine, the largest open-pit coal mine in the Americas. Approximately every second, Black Thunder mines a ton of relatively clean-burning low-sulfur coal.*

*Killed by acid rain, remnants of a forest haunt the Ore Mountains in the desolate Black Triangle region shared by the Czech Republic, Poland, and Germany. Here, in the industrial heart of Eastern Europe, the burning of high-sulfur soft coal and lignite in factories and homes has created acid rain fallout with nearly the corrosive strength of battery acid. The convoluted stacks of a cement plant near Veracruz, Mexico, help remove pollutants spawned by the manufacturing process.*

more customers without building new, often unpopular power plants.

The officers of many industries, I have observed, exhibit a defensiveness when discussing the environment with a journalist. But not the environmental champions I encountered at California's two largest utilities, Pacific Gas & Electric and Southern California Edison. The marriage of these gray-suit executives to the cause of environmentalism appeared consummated, and they seemed happy to have me along on their honeymoon.

"PG&E's efficiency programs will reduce our peak energy demand by 2,500 megawatts," said Bruce Matulich, then acting manager of energy efficiency. "This represents 75 percent of our expected demand growth for electricity for the '90s. We can meet the other 25 percent by importing electricity from the Northwest and relying on private suppliers and on renewable sources such as wind and solar. This means no need for new fossil fuel generating plants. We're all happy about that."

PG&E has weatherized more than 1.2 million homes. "A good place to see the action," suggested Mr. Matulich, "is Brentwood—our Delta Project." I hustled eastward to Brentwood, a long-time farming community between San Francisco and the San Joaquin River and burgeoning with overflow residents from the Bay Area. "To keep up with the growth," said Bruce C. Ghiselli, PG&E's Community and Customer Relations Manager and a former Brentwood mayor, "we're buying back wasted electrical capacity from established customers.

"On invitation, we go into a home and perform a pressure test to measure the efficiency of its air-conditioning duct system. Simply by tightening the air-duct system with a mastic wrapping, we can harvest kilowatt savings. We'll take you to a home we diagnosed earlier and see how much good we did there."

We drove to the home of Ron and Judy Enos. Our crew of four closed the windows and all the doors except the front. Here they placed a "blower door"—a red canvas barrier that filled the frame and held a pressure fan. The fan whirred, and pressure inside built noticeably. Busily the crew members checked an array of gauges.

"The house is leaking 2,500 cubic feet of air a minute," reported a technician. "Down 600 from before we worked on it. That's about as good as we can do. Taping the ducts stopped a quarter of the leakage. Attic insulation and window repairs helped. The biggest saving was replacing the oversize air conditioner with one tailored to the home's requirements."

"Ron and Judy Enos should see at least a 25 percent reduction on their monthly utility bill," observed Mr. Ghiselli. "PG&E harvested kilowatts toward delaying construction of that expensive substation. Emissions were cut. Multiply this a hundredfold, a thousandfold, and you make a real difference."

I flew to Los Angeles, to the campus-like headquarters of Southern California Edison, second in size only to PG&E among the nation's investor-owned utilities. Here, too, corporate executives spoke fluent environmentalese. Their conviction cascaded down from the top: In 1990, SCE elected as its chairman John E. Bryson, a co-founder of the Natural Resources

Defense Council. SCE and the neighboring Los Angeles Department of Water and Power became the first utilities in the world to pledge reductions in emissions of carbon dioxide.

# Preserving habitat

"Two of our greatest efforts," said Environmental Affairs Manager Michael M. Hertel, "go toward clean air and habitat protection. Take the latter. Our service area harbors more than a hundred threatened or endangered species of plants and animals.

"When a crew goes out to work on a transmission line or pipeline, we instruct them about threatened or endangered species in their work area." Dr. Hertel brandished SCE's thick loose-leaf book titled, *Endangered Species Alert Program Manual.* I looked up the black-tailed gnatcatcher. Environmentally this coast-dwelling cousin of the bluebird is southern California's counterpart to the northern spotted owl, causing anguish among bird-lovers and gnashing of teeth among developers.

The manual gave a brief natural history of the gnatcatcher, listed its status (candidate for the federal endangered species listing), then described potential conflicts for work crews: "Populations of this bird are very reduced due to destruction of coastal sage habitat, largely for housing developments. Any construction or maintenance activity that furthers this destruction may harm the species. Since populations are small and geographically restricted, this species is believed to be very vulnerable." A map showed the gnatcatcher's distribution in areas south of Los Angeles.

The struggle to reduce carbon dioxide emissions kindles interest in renewable energy sources, most of which do not rely on combustion. "California is the world renewables capital," said NRDC's Ralph Cavanagh. "This is primarily because its regulators and utilities have pursued them."

SCE was pursuing, hard. "Twenty-one percent of our energy comes from renewables," said Research Manager Joseph N. Reeves. "Back in 1980 we committed to using renewables to help meet our new power needs. This assisted us to make the pledge to reduce $CO_2$. We use hydro, geothermal, and windmills; 40 percent of the world's windmills feed into our grid. The technology has improved so much in the past decade that wind can now be nearly competitive with fossil fuels."

The California utilities excite worldwide attention because their innovative environmental solutions propagate across the country and around the globe. According to WRI's *1993 Environmental Almanac,* ten other states now follow California in turning to energy savings. Another innovation now spreads from the Golden State. It takes aim at our millions of old refrigerators—at their profligate waste of energy, and the menace they hold for the ozone layer.

"Old refrigerators are notoriously inefficient," said SCE's Kenneth Gudger. "One 15 years old requires at least twice the electricity of a new model. Yet when you or I buy a new fridge, we often put the old one out in the garage where it may be hot and use it for storing beer."

Another indictment came from PG&E's Gary Fernstrom: "Refrigerators are brimming with CFCs, in both the liquid coolant and the

*Sundown shimmers through strands of Spanish moss in the Florida Everglades. Some scientists predict that such subtropical conditions may spread north as far as Newfoundland unless global warming is curtailed. Deforestation and fossil fuels pour some 23 billion tons of contaminants into the atmosphere each year, trapping heat and contributing to global warming— intensifying the greenhouse effect. Destruction of the ozone layer that shields Earth from the sun's ultraviolet rays may increase the risk of skin cancer. Australian Norman Hansell, possibly a victim of overexposure to the sun, has worn an artificial nose since doctors removed a large melanoma from a nostril.*

insulation. Three-quarters is in the foam insulation that makes it so light."

In massive sweeps across much of California, the two utilities have collected thousands of old refrigerators for token payments, and slashed electricity waste. In an initiative organized by SCE, PG&E, and EPA, a number of utilities from around the nation invested more than 30 million dollars to encourage U. S. manufacturers to design, develop, and bring to the American people a super-efficient refrigerator that also is CFC free. "We needed the inducement to motivate manufacturers to build advanced models and to offset higher costs to consumers," said PG&E's Bruce Matulich. "Most buyers look first at price, features, color, and brand name before they worry about energy efficiency and ozone. We also plan to implement similar programs for energy efficient washing machines and air-conditioners."

The peril represented by ozone depletion defies comprehension for many of us. The ozone shield is one of Earth's most intangible features—an invisible scattering of oxygen molecules floating high in the stratosphere and constituting less than a hundred-thousandth of the atmosphere's total molecular content. It seems impossible that without it, life would not have emerged from the seas, and that if it vanished today, most terrestrial life would wither and die under a lethal hail of ultraviolet radiation. And that in recent decades we began destroying it wholesale. And that we still are, because of the momentum of our earlier mistakes, although we have taken dramatic remedial action that is slowly showing an effect.

Ozone forms naturally in the stratosphere when solar radiation strikes an oxygen molecule, splitting apart its paired oxygen atoms. Before the two atoms can reunite, one combines with another oxygen molecule, forming a three-atom molecule of ozone. This hefty molecule can absorb the destructive energy of the sun's ultraviolet radiation. It is a front-line soldier of the ozone shield.

For about a billion years, from the time bacteria first fortified the atmosphere with oxygen, the ozone shield performed well. Trouble brewed in the late 1920s, when scientists developed chlorofluorocarbons. In 1974 chemists F. Sherwood Rowland and Mario J. Molina calculated the pathway CFCs would follow in the atmosphere. Their conclusions drew a nightmarish scenario. The gas would rise to the stratosphere, where solar energy would break it down, freeing its chemically active chlorine atoms. A chlorine atom would capture an oxygen atom from the ozone, destroying its shield capability. Soon a solitary oxygen atom would steal the oxygen from the chlorine, and the chlorine would attack more ozone. The cycle would repeat again and again, until a single chlorine atom destroyed hundreds of ozone molecules.

Greeted initially with mixed admiration and doubt, the Rowland-Molina scenario withstood academic challenge and laboratory testing. It formed the scientific foundation for the dramatic 1987 international agreement on ozone protection known as the Montreal Protocol. Each year since, the ozone negotiators have reconvened to adjust schedules for phasing out CFCs and related ozone-depleting gases. Almost always they adjust toward more rigorous control, for the ozone shield has been sorely rent.

The shield's most gaping wound is the Antarctic ozone hole. Since its discovery in the mid-1980s, the hole has expanded almost every year. From 1991 to 1992 it grew by 15 percent to an area of nine million square miles, three times the size of the contiguous 48 states. This extends it over the populated tip of South America, including the Chilean city of Punta Arenas on the Strait of Magellan. With the enlarging of the Antarctic hole, a lesser but growing gap appeared over the Arctic. By 1991 thinning ozone was measured over high and middle latitudes of both hemispheres—in spring and summer as well as during the usual winter occurence.

Already frayed by human abuse, the fragile veil suffered nature's insult with the 1991 eruption of Mount Pinatubo in the Philippines. Tiny particles of ejected sulfur dioxide caused heating of the stratosphere over the tropics, leading to chemical reactions that reduced equatorial ozone by as much as 30 percent.

## The fate of the shield

The use of CFCs will end worldwide in January 1996, according to terms worked out by negotiators of 93 nations meeting in 1992 in Copenhagen, Denmark. The roles of CFCs will be taken over, at least transitionally, by related chemicals known as hydrochloroflurocarbons—also depleters of ozone but less virulent than CFCs. The same schedule applies to carbon tetrachloride, widely used in medicines, pesticides, and paints, and to the popular solvent, methyl chloroform. The manufacture of halons, potent ozone-destroyers used in many fire extinguishers, faced a phaseout deadline of January 1994. Developing nations, regarded as less able to shift to substitute materials, are given a ten-year grace period in phasing out the chemicals, along with help in funding replacements.

Disagreement clouds the banning of methyl bromide, a soil fumigant for agriculture believed to be responsible for about 10 percent of ozone depletion. The United States favors a cutoff by the year 2000. Developing nations and the European Community, more dependent on the chemical, won agreement to place a cap on methyl bromide starting in 1995.

Experts believe that the next 20 years are likely to see the highest atmospheric abundances of ozone-depleting gases. After that, the ozone layer could begin a gradual, natural recovery.

WRI's world emissions tables show that our total release of CFCs for 1989 was 580,000 tons. The amount is modest in comparison with the astounding burdens that fossil fuels impose on the atmosphere. Last year, worldwide burning of coal and oil emitted $CO_2$ in the amount of *22 billion* tons. Each year the world's vehicles, industrial boilers, and power plants also cough into the air a hundred million tons of sulfur and nitrogen dioxides. These are the key ingredients of acid rain.

Civilization has been aware for more than century that the sulfur and nitrogen in coal and oil combine in the air with water vapor, oxygen, and sunlight to form dilute sulfuric and nitric acids. Concern about acid rain helped launch the environmental movement, and in the United States found expression in the landmark Clean Air Act of 1970.

Properly known as acid deposition because they occur both as

Crystalline clouds high in the sky cast a ghostly glow over McMurdo Sound in Antarctica. At such stratospheric levels, ozone forms. Since the early 1970s, scientists have predicted depletion of the ozone layer. Measurements of this protective shield showed that it had thinned appreciably—a trend that continued until an actual hole was detected in 1985. The probable culprit: CFCs used as refrigerants and in aerosols that destroy ozone's effectiveness as a sunblock. In special greenhouses, scientists at the University of California, Riverside, tested the effects of air pollutants on orange trees. Tentative results suggest that ozone can lower the yields of trees and reduce fruit weight.

solids and as liquids, the wind-borne chemicals attack the works of both nature and man. The cost has been high.

The acids eat at the monuments of ancient Greece, the cathedrals and other architectural treasures of Europe, the stone and metal structures of the eastern United States. They have acidified tens of thousands of lakes and rivers in southern Norway and Sweden, thousands so severely they no longer support fish. A tenth of the lakes of the Adirondack Mountains stare skyward bright but sterile.

# The ravaged triangle

The blight of acid deposition lies with particular severity on the nations of Eastern Europe. Here, antiquated industries and coal stoves in houses often burn sulfurous soft coal and lignite, whose palls of emissions threaten health and destroy forests. The greatest damage afflicts an area known as the Black Triangle, straddling the borders of the Czech Republic, Poland, and eastern Germany.

The region is familiar terrain to Associate Professor Barrett N. Rock of the University of New Hampshire. Reconnoitering the Giant Mountains along the Czech-Polish border, he saw the effects of groundwater more acid than lemon juice. Cloud water in Poland has measured 1.8 on the pH scale, approaching the strength of battery acid. "The triangle," said Dr. Rock, "is one of the most severely polluted areas on the planet. It has no counterpart in Western Europe or the northeastern United States, both of which feel the impact of acid deposition."

Dr. Rock participates in a study—coordinated by the UN Environment Programme—of the extent and timing of the forest damage. At his laboratory in Durham, New Hampshire, he spread out satellite images of the Czech Republic's Ore Mountains for the years 1972, '78, and '85. "Earlier, I used a microscope for determining tree health," said the plant anatomist. "Now I use a 'macroscope'—the ability of satellites to extend the range of the human eye.

"Look at the '72 image—healthy forest, no strip mining. In '78 we see the beginning of the mining of lignite, which is 12 percent sulfur—terrible stuff. There are signs of forest stress, particularly along slopes at about 3,000 feet. Clouds hover at this elevation—clouds full of sulfur and other air pollutants, perhaps tropospheric ozone, the worst forest killer. I call this level the atmospheric sewer.

"Now, 1985. You can see that the forests on the upper slopes are dead. Look at the strip mining scars. Local foresters say a turning point came on New Year's Day 1978, when the temperature plunged 72° F. in 24 hours. The trees already were weakened by the pollution. The cold snap zapped them, and the forest system collapsed.

"The Czechs and the Poles have tried to reforest," said Dr. Rock. "We've looked on the ground, and most of the seedlings that we saw were dead."

What of the much publicized massive die-off of western European forests, with its ominous German name *Waldsterben*—forest death? Today the alarm sounds less shrilly, although localized diebacks exist. "Trees seem to be the part of the forest ecosystem least sensitive to air pollution," concluded Dr. J. L. Innes of the U. K. Forestry Commission at an acidification conference in the Netherlands. "Overall, [European] forest productivity has steadily increased at the regional level, which suggests that the negative effects of air pollution are overcompensated by its positive effects (nitrogen deposition) and other factors (long-term evolution of climate, increase of $CO_2$ levels, changes in silviculture practices)."

How healthy are U. S. forests? "There are areas of trouble," said Dr. Derek Winstanley, director of the National Acid Precipitation Assessment Program. "In southern California, from tropospheric ozone, and, in the Appalachians, from acid deposition at high elevations. There also is concern about sugar maples in the Northeast and Canada, although their health appears to be improving. A joint U. S.-Canadian study is tackling this. In most of the United States, however, forests enjoy good health."

Forests in the United States and Canada suffer less from acid deposition than from ozone, according to studies by forest biologist William H. Smith of Yale University. Chemically identical to the molecules of the ozone shield, tropospheric ozone forms when sunlight reacts with hydrocarbon emissions, primarily from vehicle exhausts. Vast plumes of reactive ozone drift daily from urban centers. The plumes especially damage trees downwind from the Los Angeles megalopolis and across much of the Ohio Valley and eastern seaboard.

Ozone's guilt does not exonerate acid rain. Foresters look for its danger in the future—in a long-term buildup of acidity in forest soils.

"We're shifting our interest from the direct effects of acid deposition on trees, to the indirect effect through soil chemistry," said Dr. Winstanley. "Soil acidity can slowly change. Sulfur and nitrogen pollutants can accelerate the weathering of soils and the leaching of essential trace elements such as magnesium and calcium. Metals build up, particularly those released by the burning of coal. Coal contains as much aluminum as it does sulfur, and aluminum can be highly toxic to aquatic life.

"We tend to look at air pollution problems in fragments: How do we control sulfur or nitrogen or carbon dioxide? We really should be asking how we control the source—the burning of fossil fuels."

Controls are increasing, most of them fragmentary but many meaningful. In Europe, a convention negotiated by the UN Economic Commission imposes increasingly stiff limits on emissions of sulfur dioxide and nitrogen oxide affecting sensitive forests and lakes. The European Community has mandated the fitting of new automobiles with catalytic converters and placed rigorous limits on power plant emissions.

The World Bank is helping to fund a study of the impact of acid rain in Asia, as a way of alerting governments to the damage and

*FOLLOWING PAGES: Smog, a result of the chemical reaction of sunlight on engine exhausts, casts a rush-hour pall over Los Angeles freeways. Here and elsewhere, cities try to reduce such air pollution.*

*A "voltswagon" in your future? Dr. James M. Lents, head of California's South Coast Air Quality Management District, examines cars designed to run on cleaner energy* *sources, including methanol and (with raised hoods) electric batteries. California mandates that by the year 2003, 10 percent of all new vehicles sold in the state must be electric.*

generating corrective strategies. The assessment uses a labor-saving computer model developed at Austria's International Institute for Applied Systems Analysis. Fed such data as power plant locations, emissions, rainfall patterns, and ecosystem types, the model maps where acid rain will fall and evaluates its potential damage.

Acid rain corroded a venerable international friendship—that of the United States and Canada. Lakes and forests of eastern Canada rest on granite of the Canadian Shield, which possesses little capacity for buffering the affects of acidity. Canadians saw their waters grow sterile and their woods weaken, and they blamed the troubles in part on U. S. smokestack emissions that observed no border, and fell with the rains on Canada.

Years of increasingly rancorous argument finally reached reconciliation in 1991, with the signing of the Canada-United States Air Quality Agreement. Both nations agreed to extensive reductions of acid rain emissions. The United States accepted a cap on sulfur dioxide of approximately 15 million tons a year by 2010, a 42-percent reduction from 1980 emission levels, and a nitrogen oxides reduction of two million tons below the 1980 level of 23 million tons. For Canada, the agreement calls for a reduction of sulfur dioxide emissions by 40 percent from 1980 levels in the seven easternmost provinces, to 2.3 million tons, and a commitment to reduce nitrogen oxides emissions by 100,000 tons annually.

In the United States, the struggle to combat acid deposition has been long, sometimes faltering, and very costly. Part of the problem stemmed from scientists' inability to unravel the complex causes and effects of acid rain. As a result, groping policymakers lacked a smoking gun like that which clearly linked CFCs to stratospheric ozone depletion. In the process, unprecedented stacks of reports and recommendations accumulated, and research costs across the decades climbed to half a billion dollars.

Action today flows from the 1990 amendments to the Clean Air Act, with compliance costs of several billion dollars a year.

Initial attention fixes on 110 power plants in the eastern half of the country—a collection of elderly coal burners known as the "old dirties." They must reduce sulfur emissions either by cleaning stack gases with scrubbers or by shifting to low-sulfur coal or natural gas, or they must engage in "emissions trading"—the purchase of pollution rights from plants with emission credits to sell. In the year 2000 the old dirties face still lower $SO_2$ limits, and restrictions will take effect on smaller and newer plants.

The cleanup can benefit from the Department of Energy's Clean Coal Program, which since 1987 has received five billion dollars to devise less polluting ways to burn the abundant fossil fuel. "Today's older plants are 30 to 35 percent efficient," said Dr. Winstanley. "The new, clean coal technologies raise efficiencies to 40 to 50 percent."

Irony on a Chinese boulevard: Pedal power—pollution free—carries a family's treasured new possession, a refrigerator charged with ozone-depleting CFCs. The U. S. has offered to share research into alternative refrigerants with China. In Sacramento, California, old CFC-laden refrigerators await recycling (opposite, center) under a program that offers rebates to help buy new, efficient models. A dealer helps transfer food to a new model (top); an old unit is recycled (bottom).

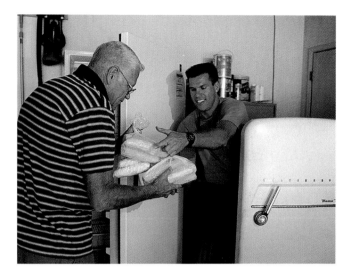

Nitrogen oxide reductions of 10 percent must be met by 2000. Nitrogen controls are low and late in arriving because nitrogen comes not only from power plants but also from vehicles. That makes it costlier to control, financially and politically.

Meanwhile, key mysteries of acid rain still elude science. "Sulfur dioxide emissions have decreased 30 percent since 1970," said Dr. Winstanley. "Yet there is little sign that the acidity of the air has decreased substantially. Or, look at the Adirondacks lakes. Despite generally rising $SO_2$ levels, since 1850 half have become *less* acidic. It's a puzzle." So complex are plant behavior and the effects of acid rain that scientists cannot yet tell exactly how acid deposition harms forest health.

If you are keeping a running score of fossil-fuel pollutants and their toll on our atmosphere, the scorecard would show $CO_2$ at 22 billion tons a year, and sulfur and nitrogen oxides at a hundred million tons. But fossil fuels hold abundances of other contaminants, including carbon monoxide, particulates, and hydrocarbons. The score for these emissions is hard to come by, but more than a quarter of a billion tons yearly escape into the levitated sludge we inhale as air. Little wonder that in cities around the world eyes sting, lungs congest, and visibility shrinks in a horizon of smog.

On my way to Amazonia, at work for this book, I visited Santiago, Chile, once a front-row seat for people admiring its eastern backdrop of snow-clad Andean peaks. This time a curtain of contaminants hid them completely, even though the striving city enforced a rotating schedule that kept a fifth of the cars off the streets each day.

Smog often veils São Paulo and Rio de Janeiro in Brazil; Bombay and Delhi in India; Athens, Greece; Lisbon, Portugal; and Milan, Italy. Particularly severe conditions hang over coal-burning Chinese cities, such as Xian, Beijing, and Shanghai; industrial Benxi so pollutes its air that satellite sensors no longer detect it beneath a toxic shroud. Breathing Mexico City's air is compared to smoking two packs of cigarettes a day. Air quality is cited as a major health hazard in scores of Russian cities and in the Black Triangle of the Czech Republic, Poland, and Germany. A study by the World Health Organization and the UN Environment Programme found that more than 600 million of the world's urbanites live in levels of sulfur dioxide considered by WHO to be excessive.

In the United States, substantial attention and funding are slowly cleansing the air of six pollutants: carbon monoxide, nitrogen dioxide, ozone, lead, particulates, and sulfur dioxide. Nevertheless, EPA finds that some 80 million Americans live in areas with air that is at times unhealthy.

To measure the quality of the air we breathe, EPA receives periodic reports on the targeted pollutants from nearly 4,100 monitoring sites across the nation, most operated by state and local governments. Despite growing numbers of autos and industrial plants, the readings show that during the past decade pollution concentrations declined significantly for all except nitrogen oxide. In recent years it too has beaten a reluctant retreat.

The weapon that wins these grudging gains is the Clean Air Act. Passed initially in 1970 and amended in 1977 and 1990, the CAA costs

Americans about 60 billion dollars a year. The investment, borne largely by industry and passed on to consumers, has bought improvements such as scrubbers on smokestacks, catalytic converters on cars, vapor guards at gas stations, and the removal of lead from gasoline.

Despite the gains, many counties fail to comply with federal air quality standards for one or more of the pollutants on one or more days a year. Not surprisingly, these "nonattainment" areas hold major cities: Houston, Denver, New York, Philadelphia, Washington, D. C. In all but New York City, whose number one problem is carbon monoxide, the leading pollutant is usually ozone, primarily the product of vehicle exhausts.

The Los Angeles area is in a class by itself. With its eastern wall of mountains trapping the air, with 9 million motor vehicles and 30,000 industries and 13 million citizens, with abundant sunshine cooking pollutants into rich chemical brews, the teeming Los Angeles Basin and surrounding counties endure by far the dirtiest air in the nation. This despite air pollution controls that are the world's tightest—and growing tighter.

At the environmental command post of the South Coast Air Quality Management District, six and a half feet of harassed executive stood silhouetted at a cafeteria window. "It's a good day," said James M. Lents, looking out appreciatively. "You can see the mountains." You could; only a faint haze softened the 11,000-foot crests of the San Bernardino and San Gorgonio Mountains, looking down on the busy Route 10 Freeway.

Unremarkable in virtually any other setting, the shimmering air beyond the glass meant hope to the embattled Dr. Lents. Since his arrival in 1986, the 13 million people who inhabit his district have seen their ozone air quality improve 50 percent, the most for any major metropolitan area. The district now meets federal standards for sulfur dioxide and lead, and is closing in on nitrogen oxide. But there has been a negative side. Corrective measures have not been cheap, businesses have fled, jobs left with them, and residents have chafed at restraints ranging from enforced carpooling to curbing emissions from fast-food drive-ins. Dr. Lents was feeling the heat.

The strict measures also were infringing on the vaunted California lifestyle. "We've had to restrict home activities—the use of barbecue starter fluid, hair sprays, underarm spray deodorant," said Dr. Lents. "They may seem trivial, but when millions of people do something, it adds up.

"I worry about health effects of air pollution. Studies show that area children have 15 percent less lung function than kids from Houston— a city with its own air problems. Autopsies show lesions on the lungs of young nonsmokers."

## Selling pollution credits

The flight of business from the region helped shape an innovation known as the regional clean air incentives market, or RECLAIM. "If a company reduces its emissions below the standard required, it can sell the pollution credit to another firm," explained Dr. Lents. "This shifts clean air from regulatory decree to marketable commodity. Air quality officials around the world are watching."

I descended to a basement air-quality laboratory, one of the largest

"I'm not interested in doing with less, but in doing more with less," claims Amory Lovins, a physicist who induced California utility companies to adopt energy-efficient practices, including solar (above) and wind alternative energy sources. His latest brainchild: a hybrid fuel-and-electric car with a range of about 300 miles per gallon.

FOLLOWING PAGES: On a "wind farm" in California's Tehachapi Mountains, high-tech turbines provide enough clean, efficient power to supply the household needs of a city the size of San Francisco.

in the world. Chemists and other scientists tended phalanxes of computerized air analyzers. "We chase the main offenders—hydrocarbons, particulates, and oxides of nitrogen," said principal chemist Steven Barbosa.

Mr. Barbosa showed me a filter from a particulates monitor in Long
Beach for September 9. It wore a coating of gray-black dust, but measured
well within federal and state standards. "Particles rise from the area's
refineries, from the 405 Freeway, from ships and trucks and cars. The
onshore winds bear them east over the city, where they collide with other
particles, grow larger, and create a soupy, grayish haze in the sky. The sul-
fate particles merge until they're just the right size to scatter the light and
create our white haze." How was he doing, this soldier in a science bunker?
"We're learning more about the pollutants, how to control them. We're
winning the war."

To solve southern California's air quality problem, and that of Mexico City and Santiago and Athens and choking cities everywhere,
experts know they must vanquish the emissions that escape the
automobile tailpipe. These supply the hydrocarbons and nitrogen
oxides that react with sunlight to produce ozone, public enemy
number one in urban air pollution.

To clean up the tailpipe, the South Coast group is testing a large
fleet of cars powered by methanol, a promising alcohol fuel. The California Air Resources Board mandates doing away with the tailpipe
altogether. The means for this is the electric vehicle, a pet project of the
enthusiasts at Southern California Edison.

"California regulation," said Richard Schweinberg at utility headquarters, "requires the the gradual phasing in of zero-emission vehicles—
and that means electric: 2 percent of new vehicle sales starting in 1998,
5 percent by 2001, 10 percent by 2003. That 10 percent means some 200,000
vehicles, so we're talking about lots of passenger cars. A dozen other states
are considering similar requirements. Electric vehicles could reduce emissions here 97 percent, if gasoline vehicles are replaced.

"The hang-up, of course, is the batteries. Lead-acid batteries for a
full-size van weigh 1,200 pounds and have a range of only 60 miles. We've
teamed up with other utilities, the big auto manufacturers, and the Department of Energy to push battery research. One company has a new-
generation nickel battery that looks twice as good as lead, and could be in
production within several years." What about recharging? "We have
enough surplus nighttime generating capacity to recharge more than one
million cars," said Mr. Schweinberg with relish. "We're also developing a
carport with solar-powered recharge capability."

With Suzan Sines as copilot, I climbed behind the wheel of Southern California Edison's demonstrator electric van, with a license plate that
read SMG FRE 1. I turned the key and listened for the engine to cough to
life: Stupid—an electric motor runs only when the car is moving. My eye
sought the usual dashboard gauges: Stupid—these blissfully simple
machines require a single "charge" gauge. Chastened, I adroitly shifted to
D (no first and second gears, you know) and accelerated smoothly into a
SMG FRE future.

# The Face of the EARTH

To humans, the most important event on Earth each year probably is the harvest. In this colossal drama, a cast of billions goes forth into the fields to gather an often hard-won bounty. The largest part is grain, life's staple—of this they reap 1.7 billion tons a year. Were they to bring it all together at the Equator, it would build a highway of grain sixty feet wide and seven and a half feet thick, stretching for 27,000 miles around the world.

This effort to feed ourselves requires tillage and grazing on a scale that has utterly transformed a major part of our terrestrial environment. If you picture Earth's virgin landscape as a great blackboard, with the plants and animals of the

*A staff of life since the beginnings of agriculture, wheat nods bristly heads. Cereal grains, such as wheat, rice, and corn, supply half of the calories consumed worldwide.*

natural environment chalked in, you could say that farming has wiped across it like a giant eraser. The farmed environment is a transformed environment—a blackboard erased, then rewritten by the hand of humankind.

With the human population growing faster than ever before, more and more wild land succumbs to plow and cow. Environmentalists look with particular alarm at the rapid loss of two types of terrain, both of them vital ecosystems rich in diversity of life: tropical forests and wetlands.

Tropical forests are under assault around the world. Once they covered about four billion acres of Africa, Asia, and South and Central America. Today only about half still stand, and they are falling at a quickening pace—to agriculture, as well as fuel gathering, logging, and development such as dam impoundments. Southern Asia and its galaxy of archipelagoes, which once held perhaps a fifth of the planet's moist tropical forest, is disappearing the most rapidly. Central and West Africa held about a third; today most of the West African forests have toppled, though the great Zairean rain forest remains largely intact. Most of the rest of the world's tropical rain forest cloaks the mountainous spine of Central America—where three-fifths has vanished—and the northern half of South America.

The heart of that South American forest is the expanse known as Amazonia. The 2.7 million square miles drained by the world's mightiest river have become a focus of global concern—"the symbol of the environment," in the words of Dr. Thomas E. Lovejoy, Assistant Secretary of the Smithsonian Institution and an innovator of measures to protect the region.

In his office at the Smithsonian's old brick "castle," Dr. Lovejoy spread out a map and pointed to Brazil. "Deforestation forms a crescent," he explained, "from Belém at the mouth of the river southward and then westward all the way across the country to Bolivia—more than 2,000 miles. When I began working in Amazonia 28 years ago, two million people were thinly scattered about the region, living largely in areas made accessible by rivers. Now there are 17 million inhabitants, living largely along new roads."

But so huge is the forest that it is still surprisingly intact. Because of the area's vastness, measurements proved difficult to make. Only satellites, hundreds of miles above Earth, can view such a landscape on a proper scale. And even satellite sensors cannot penetrate the cloud cover that frequently obscures much of the Amazon basin.

For two decades, however, Brazil has operated a sophisticated space agency. As reports of alarming destruction reached the world, and foreign nations criticized Brazil, the Brazilian government directed the agency to conduct a careful monitoring program.

The agency's report for the period 1978-88 gave an annual cutting rate of about five million acres a year—much lower than most outside authorities believed. This provoked claims that the Brazilian measurements were self-serving and that the rate was much higher.

Because the rate of deforestation affects the global release of carbon dioxide and global warming, NASA was also in the fray, funding a study by the University of New Hampshire which undertook a massive review of all available satellite imagery of Amazonia. To learn the result,

I visited the University of New Hampshire's Institute for the Study of Earth, Oceans, and Space.

"We sorted through two million images from the U. S. Landsat satellites, looking for coverage that was cloud free," said Dr. David Skole. "Eventually we located 240 clear images that form a mosaic of the Brazilian Amazon for the years 1978-88. The U. S. and Brazilian studies showed a rate of cutting much lower than anyone else had claimed—it ranged from about 3.7 to 5 million acres a year." In all, according to the University of New Hampshire, about 6 percent. Compared to most of the rest of the world, the Brazilian Amazon seems to have escaped lightly.

"What's saved the Amazon," explained Bruce Nelson of Brazil's National Institute for Research in the Amazon, "is the difficulty of making a living here." I visited the botanist and his wife Sherre at their home in Manaus, queen city of Amazonia.

"Unlike many northern forests, which grow in lands recently scoured by Ice Age glaciers, the rain forest has evolved over millions of years and acquired a great diversity," said Mr. Nelson. "This diversity—hundreds of different tree species in a single hectare, or about two and a half acres—until recently discouraged logging, which profits most from dense stands of a single species."

But there have been moneymaking schemes aplenty. Virtually all have been at the expense of the first occupants, the Indians.

## Roads and settlement

Brazil saw a rubber boom from the 1880s to the early 1900s, although it made little impact on the rain forest. That came in the late 1950s, when Brazil built an all-weather highway connecting Belém with the new national capital, Brasília. Settlers by the hundreds of thousands poured onto the highway and staked claims along its 1,200-mile length. Many aimed to be subsistence farmers; many more sought land for pasturing cattle and for speculation, for which the government gave enticing subsidies.

This pattern—new road followed by a wave of settlement—repeated itself in the next decades as other highways penetrated Amazonia. The longest, the 3,480-mile Trans-Amazon Highway, begun in 1970, thrust from Brazil's easternmost cities of Recife and João Pessoa to the western border with Peru; government propaganda touted it as "connecting people with no land to a land with no people"—a contention that forest Indian tribes frequently and forcibly disputed.

In the late '80s, reports came out of Amazonia of immense clouds of smoke—smoke hanging over virtually the entire basin. Astronauts 150 miles overhead in the space shuttle brought back confirming photographs—smoke spreading like an overcast from the Atlantic to the distant Andes.

*FOLLOWING PAGES: Steers fatten in a Utah feedlot after rangeland grazing. Meat production greatly alters the environment, both for pasturage and feed grain. Worldwide, almost 40 percent of harvested grain goes to feed livestock; in the U. S., it is nearly 70 percent.*

Analysis of satellite images revealed 7,603 fires in a single day. They could only mean the clearing and burning of forest on a massive scale.

Like enormous smoke signals, the fires drew world attention, this time to Rondônia. For about ten years a dirt road connecting the capitals of the states of Rondônia and Mato Grosso had drawn settlers. In 1981, Brazil received loans of 432 million dollars from the World Bank, paved the highway—BR-364—and promised to protect the Indians and the environment.

By the time the paving was completed, in 1984, hard times elsewhere in Brazil had created massive unemployment. A tidal wave of impoverished settlers swept into Rondônia—150,000 newcomers a year. They overwhelmed the promised safeguards, and embarked on a holocaust of clearing and burning. By the time the influx abated  at the end of the decade, 20 percent of the state had been torched and settled as farm or pasture—then, in many cases, abandoned. Although the forest soils support some of the densest plant growth on Earth, they lack the available nutrients to sustain agricultural productivity. Today's colonists, unable to support themselves in one place for more than a year or two, and far too numerous to allow the forest to recover as in the past, relentlessly gnaw at the receding forest, leaving behind a vast landscape of spent soils.

What promise can these stubborn lands offer? I found an answer at the experimental center of the Brazilian Agricultural Research Corporation in the far western state of Acre. "Brazil has about 15 million hectares of deforested land that once was pasture and now is abandoned to secondary growth," said Dr. Mario Dantas. "This is enough land to feed Brazil's expanding population for decades, if we can make it productive.

"The new approach, known as agroforestry, attempts to mimic the rain forest itself. It uses a multistoried mix of annual staples such as corn, rice, beans, and cassava, combined with perennial shrubs and trees that provide fruits, nuts, medicinals, fibers, even fuelwood and timber. The mix is geared to meet household and market needs, as well as the demands of soil and climate. The key is a high diversity of plants."

Diversity reigned in the center's thousand acres of test plots. Dr. Dantas pointed out nurseries of palms and coffee trees, tangerines and mangoes, brazil nuts and bananas. We saw a planting of the guarana, its seeds hanging on tendrils from the fruit and grotesquely resembling eyeballs. Corn, tomatoes, cabbages, cassava, rice, pineapples. A grove of cashew trees, badly mangled ("Our experimental water buffalo got into those"). Several black pepper plantings—a good cash crop. Forty varieties of kudzu, high in protein but an aggressive plant. "None of our systems rely on fertilizers," said Dr. Dantas. "They're too expensive for frontier agriculture."

With the ending of government subsidies for cattle ranching and a new caution about colonization, Brazil's inroads into the rain forest have

*A dune threatens to overwhelm a pasture in Niger's Sahel, a semiarid belt south of the Sahara. In the last 50 years, drought, overgrazing, and deforestation have helped the desert spread, but, with controlled grazing programs—and sufficient rain— much desertified land could recover.*

*Covered head-to-toe in protective clothing, California field hands spray pesticides on ripening strawberries.*

*Poisons kill harmful insects—but also beneficial ones, including microbes that promote soil fertility.*

slackened. "Now, with an infrastructure of highways well established, and timber prices rising sharply," observed Dr. Christopher Uhl of Pennsylvania State University, "the new actor in the forest is the lumberman."

Supported in part with funding from the National Geographic Society, Dr. Uhl has devoted a career to research into forest regrowth and the impact of selective logging and burning. With Brazilian colleagues, he has analyzed the Brazilian logging industry where it operates the most frenziedly, in the eastern Amazonian county of Paragominas.

Paragominas lies in northern Pará, a state long bisected by the early Belém-Brasília Highway. Along this road the forces of forest destruction have been at work the longest. Three-quarters of the nation's roundwood is harvested from this most deforested of Brazil's Amazonian states. Paragominas, a robust frontier town, is the hub of that deforestation.

My bus for Paragominas followed the Belém-Brasília Highway. Between the towns stretched large fazendas, or ranches, many with substantial homes, cattle, and plantations of palms, citrus, bananas, and nut trees. An occasional sawmill crouched amid stacks of logs. After a few hours, the air grew hazy. Billows of smoke appeared—gray mixed with black. On each side of the highway, land was afire, some being cleared of scrub that had been bulldozed and windrowed, some with fires whipping

*Instead of spraying, this organic farmer lets his geese do the weeding on a strawberry farm in Washington's Skagit Valley. By avoiding expensive pesticides, farmers can often lower costs and enhance soil productivity.*

through second-growth forest—both being burned to improve pasture.

Eventually the sweet smell of newly cut wood mingled with the eye-watering smoke. Sawmills appeared at the roadsides…then more sawmills…dozens of them. Trucks loaded with logs sped past, stirring clouds of pink dust. Lumber kilns and charcoal ovens radiated heat and smoke. No road signs were needed to announce Paragominas.

I joined Paulo Barreto, a youthful forest engineer and colleague of Dr. Uhl. We drove to a rise at the edge of town. A mosaic of sawmills filled the view. "Most of the lumber is used here in Brazil," said Paulo. "Only about 10 percent is exported." Amid stacks of lumber, charcoal ovens shaped like igloos simmered under wisps of smoke. The charcoal would go to iron smelters at Carajás to the south.

We drove over dusty dirt roads plied by processions of laden logging trucks, and entered a battered-looking forest. "It's being selectively cut," said Paulo. "The loggers here utilize about a hundred species of trees, and they are not gentle with the forest."

We passed a succession of small clearings. "Log loading areas," explained Paulo. "The crews abandon one and clear another as they work back into the forest." We pushed to the front of the cutting. We watched hypnotized as a giant tree toppled and crashed to the forest floor in a torrent of dislodged leaves and branches. A logger with a machete walked the length of the felled tree, slashing away limbs and measuring the great bole with a meter stick. Periodically he cut a notch. Behind, a man with a chain saw stopped at each notch and sectioned the tree.

A powerful skidder roared to life and charged the tree, steel jaws gaping, a spare chain saw snapped to one side like a saddle gun. The monster snapped up a log, spun, and tore through the forest to a clearing.

Paulo and I moved to a quiet spot, where another tree had been felled and already hauled out. Several other large trees had lost their crowns, snapped off by the falling tree and the vines that had festooned it. The bulldozer and skidding log also had taken a toll. "That's the terrible waste in current cutting practices," he said. "Our study showed that for each tree they log, they kill or damage 27 more. The removal of a few logs per hectare destroys 40 or 50 percent of the forest cover. But simple practices we are teaching can reduce this loss by as much as half."

A growing fear accompanies the widespread logging: fear that it is turning the region into a tinderbox. Cutting litters the forest floor with slash and opens the canopy; sunlight dries the slash. In the dry season, logged ecosystems represent a new fire environment in Amazonia.

It was dry when I visited the Paragominas area. Often smoke drew a veil across the cloudless sky. At high noon, with Paulo Barreto, I watched the torching of a field on which the scrub had been bulldozed into piles. Each of 11 workmen—fazenda cowboys—carried a yard-long stick tipped with a swatch of rubber tire that burned fiercely. With a brisk wind blowing and the sun blazing down, the men spread out and thrust their torches into piles of brush that exploded into flames. Soon the entire field roiled with wind-whipped fire. Next to it stood a tract of logged forest, its floor strewn with the tinder of dried slash....

What happens to land that is deforested, then abandoned? Does the forest return? Or does sunlight chemically change the exposed soil so it resists revegetating? Research on fields of the Fazenda Vitoria, near Paragominas, has done much to answer those questions.

"The recovery of forest on land that has been cleared and abandoned is determined by the intensity of the use the land received before abandonment," said Dr. Daniel C. Nepstad of the Woods Hole Research Center. "The notion of desertification—that the forest, once cut, never reestablishes itself—does not hold. To the contrary, many ranchers have difficulty maintaining grass cover because of the tenacity with which trees sprout from residual roots and seeds."

From the planet's largest tropical rain forest, I traveled to its largest temperate rain forest, the great belt of conifers that lies like a green shag rug along the Pacific slopes of North America. Only a fraction as large as Amazonia, and possessed of far fewer species, the majestic forests that stretch from California to Alaska engender no less passion among those who would use them and those who would save them. They also provoke charges of hypocrisy from foreign observers who compare the conservation advice we give others with our confusion over saving our own rain forest.

Nine-tenths of the temperate rain forest of the United States is gone, devoured by domestic markets and loaded onto ships of Asian nations of the Pacific Rim. The scream of the chain saws escalated, particularly during the 1980s, in both the western United States and British Columbia.

As the timbering increased, so did opposition to it. Much of what was being cut was seen not merely as trees, but as a national treasure that had been centuries in the making. These are the controversial "old growth": California's sequoias, the largest trees on Earth, and the state's coastal redwoods, the tallest; the majestic Douglas firs of Oregon and Washington; the spruce and fir of British Columbia; the dense stands of Sitka spruce cloaking the Alaskan Panhandle. The logging also threatened wildlife habitat.

The ugly tensions of jobs versus environment eventually entered the courts. They forced far-reaching legal decisions that could restructure the relationship between resources and ecosystems. The hottest battles raged in the Pacific Northwest of the United States, and in British Columbia, where half of Canada's timber is harvested.

Many sawmills were quiet, local economies sorely hurting, when I visited old-growth country in Oregon. I stopped in Eugene, gateway to the national forests that ride the Oregon Cascades like a saddle blanket. Today the national forests and other federal and state lands hold virtually all the remaining 5.7 million acres of coastal old growth in the U. S. Northwest; almost all on private holdings has been cut.

# Old growth versus timber jobs

Eugene appeared quiet on the surface, but underneath antagonisms were seething like the innards of Mount St. Helens. From their office on Briarcliffe Lane, environmentalists Tim and Deborah Hermach of the Native Forest Council were campaigning to protect the hard-pressed remaining monarch trees. Across town on Charnelton Street, I called on Jeff DeBonis. For 12 years a timber-sale planner for the Forest Service, Jeff had rebelled against the rampant cutting of the 1980s and turned to organizing support from others within the service who were disillusioned.

I entered a burger establishment and struck up a conversation with retired timber-industry mechanic Jack Seymore. He stoutly defended the practices of loggers, and deplored the excesses of environmentalism. "Excuse me," came a voice from the next booth: "I overheard." He joined us—a young family man who had worked at the giant Weyerhaeuser plant at the edge of town. "I was an edger at the sawmill," he said, "until they closed it down. Timber got too expensive, what with that crazy dispute about the owl."

"The owl" is, of course, *Strix occidentalis*     (Continued on page 102)

*FOLLOWING PAGES: Terraced rice fields scallop a slope on the tropical island of Bali. Here, centuries-old irrigation systems produce as many as three harvests a year. One of the world's major food crops, rice provides a staple diet for roughly half the people on Earth.*

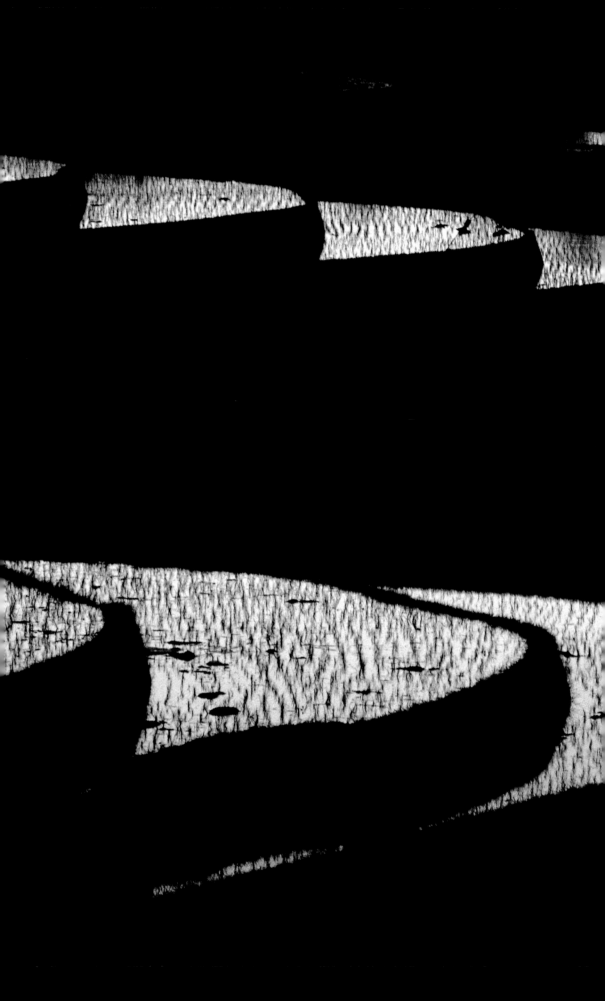

*Revolution in the making: Rows of cotton flourish under irrigation on an experimental farm near Fresno, California. The foreground field— conventionally flooded—requires far more water than distant fields, irrigated by buried plastic tubing that feeds directly to roots. This type of subsurface drip irrigation was devised by Claude J. Phene (opposite), a scientist with the U. S. Department of Agriculture. Because Dr. Phene's system is underground, it does not lose moisture to evapora- tion, thus minimizing the salt buildup that can ruin irrigated fields. Using Dr. Phene's method, a nearby grape grower has been able to double his yield with only half the water other growers use.*

*caurina,* the northern spotted owl. Perhaps 3,000 to 5,000 pairs of the owls survive in the remaining monarch forest in Oregon and Washington, prey-ing on flying squirrels and red tree voles. Research in the 1980s revealed that the hunting range of a pair of owls covers an enormous area—3,000 to 5,000 acres or more—of shrinking forest.

This discovery, seized upon by environmentalists and embodied in lawsuits, prompted the U. S. Fish and Wildlife Service to add the bird to its list of threatened species. Citing the rigorous requirements of the Endan-gered Species Act, a Seattle federal judge barred further timber sales on federal lands until the Fish and Wildlife Service brought forth a plan for protecting the owl and other threatened, old-growth species. When I reached the Northwest, cutting on public lands had shriveled to stands sold before the decision.

To learn of the dispensation won by the owl, I called on Dr. E. Charles Meslow at Oregon State University in Corvallis, an authority on the bird. In 1989, Dr. Meslow helped prescribe a plan for owl survival. He showed me a report, hot off the press, then unrolled a map of western Ore-gon. Between the crest of the Cascades and the Pacific coast, the map showed some 40 shaded areas, each irregular in shape, each numbered.

"These are owl habitat reserves," said Dr. Meslow. "There are sim-ilar maps for Washington and northern California. Each reserve is on fed-eral land. Wherever possible, each is large enough to support 20 or more pairs of owls. These should be able to maintain themselves through all adversities, such as heavy snows and die-offs of their prey. Notice the close-ness of one preserve to the next? They're spaced so that a young owl from one unit has a reasonable chance of locating a neighboring unit.

"The reserves take up about a quarter of all the land controlled by the Forest Service and the Bureau of Land Management west of the Cascades," said Dr. Meslow. "By setting up the reserve pattern, we think we have taken care of the needs of many of the birds and other animals associated with old-growth forests."

What about the old growth that lies on federal lands outside the reserves? In Oregon and Washington this portion is large—some 2.6 million acres. It is the portion controlled by the American public, through Congress and its agents, the Forest Service and the BLM.

Because the Forest Service and the BLM sell leases for cutting, and thus deal directly with the companies with the chain saws, the role of the Congress receives less attention. But the Congress is key. Each year, after receiving recommendations from the two agencies, it votes on "the cut," the number of board feet that will be taken the next year from federal lands. Almost invariably, the recommended cut, which conservationists usually regard as already too high, is increased at the request of Northwest law-makers, whose states and communities benefit from logging jobs and tax revenues. This expanded quota goes out to the Forest Service and the BLM as an edict they must obey through timber sales.

In separate deliberations, the Congress regulates the Forest Service and the BLM management of the forests—regulations the agencies then interpret. Significant change has marked this management across the decades, and recent changes attempt to minimize the impact of logging on

*A newly cut road scars a wilderness tract on the island of Sumatra in Indonesia. Demand for tropical hardwoods today threatens many of the world's rain forests.*

*FOLLOWING PAGES: Fire and smoke mark a pyre for a swath of virgin forest in Rondônia, Brazil, where vast interior areas have been cleared by farmers, ranchers, and miners.*

ecosystems. New logging techniques strive to mimic the disturbances such as lightning-caused fire, landslides, and disease that forests undergo naturally, and recover from. These events, even when severe, leave standing and fallen trees—legacies of surviving biological organisms and nutrients that set the damaged ecosystem on the path to recovery.If scientists could pattern tree harvests after the natural disturbances, the reasoning went, the human-caused disturbances could enjoy similar recoveries.

# Lessons from nature

As a testing ground for the new techniques, the Forest Service chose the Willamette National Forest in the Cascades. On a stormy winter morning, I groped eastward from Eugene to the H. J. Andrews Experimental Forest, where for 45 years scientists have conducted some of the most important studies ever made of forest ecosystems and their protection.

"I'll introduce you to the old growth first," said Dr. W. Arthur McKee, a forestry science professor at Oregon State who for 15 years has used the Andrews as a lab. We slogged through snow two feet deep to the banks of Lookout Creek, studied for decades to learn the effects of logging on stream chemistry and organisms. My eye fixed on a mighty column sheathed in brown, scaly bark and followed it upward—up 100 feet, 200, until its crown vanished in swirling snow clouds. It was a Douglas fir perhaps 400 years in the growing, to me a miracle of creation, to some, raw material for half a dozen modest homes. Monarchs of similar antiquity rose beside it, clustered like pilings for supporting the leaden sky above us.

Dr. McKee shook the snow from the branch of a small tree. "This is the renowned Pacific yew. The bark holds a long-chain alcohol molecule, taxol, that offers a defense against some cancers." The yew's miraculous healing properties created a demand that threatened its survival in the forest, but now taxol is being synthesized.

We clambered into a SnoCat and chugged up a mountain trail. At a promontory overlooking a precipitous gorge, Dr. McKee stopped. "On the slopes across from us," he said, "we see different methods of logging— one area clear-cut, burned, and replanted the old way, and another area logged the new way, leaving the slash and snags and some downed logs and standing green trees—the legacies. Over the years we will monitor the ecological recovery of both tracts: the species changes of plants and animals; their biomass; microclimates; water chemistry, temperature, and volume; soil chemistry and erosion; wood production; structure of the canopy.

"We expect the managed ecosystem tract to do better in almost every category. If you want to preserve biodiversity *and* harvest wood, we think we can do that. The wood harvest in the short term is reduced by 5 to 25 percent, and this bothers some of the companies. But in this district, ecosystem management is now required with all cutting. Other areas are adopting it, as are some private timber owners."

With Jim Freeman, a former Forest Service firefighter who 15 years ago became a forest aviator, I sought an aerial view of old-growth country. Taking off from Eugene into a gray, overcast sky, we lifted over the Coburg Hills and their renowned nudist colony—scarcely worth ogling from 4,000 feet. Steam rose from the Weyerhaeuser plant, and from huge mills owned by International Paper and Georgia Pacific. Fresh snow whitened the rising slopes of the Cascades.

Following the gorge of the McKenzie River, we reached the Willamette, with the Umpqua National Forest to the south. The scene below resembled a giant quilt—blocks of snow-whitened logged areas intermingled with the gray-green of standing forest. This was the patchwork pattern left by logging along most of the great arc of the temperate rain forest.

Jim pointed down at a steep slope. "Helilogging," he said. "It's horrendously expensive, but it's easier on the environment." Far below, a powerful dual-rotor helicopter hovered while two antlike figures—a choker setter and a hook tender—lashed a dangling cable around waiting logs. Quickly the copter rose and bore its swinging burden to a roadside drop point, where a third ant, known as a chaser, freed the clutch of logs.

A sprinkling of trees still stood on the newly cut unit, outlined against the white of the shorn slope. These were the standing "green trees" that Willamette loggers now must leave to help forest recovery. Snow hid the leavings of downed logs and slash—all bridges to future growth.

"See that line of trees at the bottom of the slope?" Jim Freeman asked. "They were left to protect a creek—that's called a riparian zone."

I asked what impressed him most after 15 years of flying the forest. "When I began, I was amazed at how much had been cut. Now, after all the ruckus you hear, I'm amazed at how much forest is left."

There is a northern forest that dwarfs all others on Earth, even the mighty tropical rain forest of Amazonia. Within its boundaries lie half of the world's coniferous trees, a quarter of all its forest of any type. It is the great forest of Russia. It marches in a broad sweep from the Pacific coast of Siberia westward to span the Asian continent. Dominated by pine, spruce, larch, and fir, and punctuated with birch and aspen, this great green splash on the planet has seen only a tiny fraction of its stands fall to ax and chainsaw. But the rate of destruction is quickening as three powerful forces take their toll.

The first is increased logging. Russia wants to sell wood for hard currency. Much of the wood from eastern forests is going to the Japanese, North and South Koreans, and Europeans. The Russians have heavily exploited the forests from Lake Baikal westward to Novosibirsk, mainly for domestic use.

Fires, too, cause losses. Russian forests fuel the planet's largest holocausts. "Analyzing the satellite images, I can see a loss of 2 or 3 percent of Russia's Yana River basin forests to fire each year," said Thomas Stone of the Woods Hole Research Center. "The fires probably are natural, usually from lightning, and the Russians are unable to suppress most of them. This could grow worse with global warming." But there is an interest in fire detection and prevention technology.

Human-caused stresses are another factor. Experts suggest that pollution could be part of the problem in the poor regeneration of Russian forests, and that logging methods may compact the soil. Also, harvesting may cause the permafrost to melt, changing the microclimates.

Barometer of change, the threatened northern spotted owl thrives in the shrinking old-growth forests that rim the Pacific coast of the United States. Giant firs, cedars, spruce, and hemlocks—many of them hundreds of years old—grow in these virgin woodlands. Lumbermen, such as this logger near Beaver Cove, British Columbia (opposite), value old-growth trees for their knot-free, straight-grain timber.

Compared to the majesty and romance found in forests, Earth's wetlands have languished as poor relations. Until recently, little heed was given as these undramatic swamps and marshes were drained for agriculture, diked for rice and indigo and aquaculture, filled for development, and drilled for oil.

Today new respect attaches to these priceless moist reaches. We recognize them as prime producers of life, some twice as fecund as rain forest; as custodians of large stocks of carbon that otherwise could contribute to global warming; as the feeding, spawning, and nursery grounds for perhaps half our annual harvest of finfish and shellfish; as the habitat of countless resident and migrant bird species and myriad plants and other animals; as filters of contaminants that would degrade our waters; as sponges for potential floodwaters and stabilizers of shorelines and riverbanks; as rechargers of our aquifers.

# Wetlands in peril

Wetlands today cover about 6 percent of Earth's land surface. Tomorrow that number will be slightly lower, for they have proved to be among the most difficult landforms to protect.

Earth's largest wetland is the Pantanal in Brazil. "Unfortunately, the Pantanal is the sinkhole of central Brazil, in that toxic chemicals and sediments wash in from higher agricultural lands around it," said Dr. Russell Mittermeier, president of Conservation International. "Fortunately, some local landowners realize the value of their environment and have begun to band together to protect it."

In Africa, wetlands are the major sources of protein for the continent's fast-growing human population. Marshes ringing Lake Chilwa on the Malawi-Mozambique border support an intensive fishery. In Mali, the annual flooding of the inner delta of the Niger River spreads nutrient-rich waters onto more than 7,000 square miles of parched desert to provide indispensable forage for 2.5 million head of livestock, habitat for 90 percent of the nation's fish catch, and rich, moist soils for millet, sorghum, and rice. Seasonal flooding of Cameroon's Logone River gave similar benefits—until the cycle was destroyed by construction of the Maga Dam for irrigation. Worldwide attention focuses on development plans threatening Botswana's Okavango, one of the largest inland deltas in the world. Its annual inundations today sustain perhaps the mightiest remaining refuge of large African animals. Plans to open a titanium mine in the spectacular St. Lucia wetlands of South Africa are likely to be approved despite public protests.

The greatest aggregation of wetlands sparkles across glacier-scoured Canada. In turn, Canada has included the greatest acreage in the List of Wetlands of International Importance—vast tracts that sprinkle the nation from Newfoundland to the Yukon.

Time has not been kind to the wetlands of the United States. At the nation's birth, 220 million acres of swamp and marsh lay across the lower 48 states; today more than half have vanished, and those remaining succumb at a rate of some 300,000 acres a year despite protective laws. An exception to this sad story is Alaska, where immense expanses of tundra and other wetlands total 170 million acres.

Other than in Alaska, the nation's major wetlands lie in Florida and along the lower Mississippi River, primarily in Louisiana. In the West, California's Central Valley once held extensive wetlands. Encompassing 13 million acres, the Central Valley nurtured nearly 5 million acres of wetlands, largely along the Sacramento and San Joaquin Rivers and at their delta. They hosted migratory birds of the Pacific flyway, as well as greater sandhill cranes, white-faced ibis, black-crowned night herons, great and snowy egrets, and numerous smaller birds.

As the great gold rush of 1849 drew hordes to nugget-strewn rivers above the valley, Californians also began manipulating the valley floor—the water, desert, and wetlands—to shape what would become the world's most productive agricultural area. Wetlands, competing with agriculture for space and water, lost big—about 95 percent are now erased.

What is the status of the land itself—the soil that grows our crops and holds our precious groundwater—the very ground beneath our feet? In its global assessment of soil conditions, the World Resources Institute paints a grim picture. At a time of inexorably escalating population and food needs, WRI finds that more than three billion acres "have been significantly degraded since World War II." Many experts dispute the severity of such widespread degradation, but all see a problem.

The 15 percent of tilled land that is in irrigation produces a whopping third of the global harvest. Many of the most populous countries are the most irrigated: China, India, Indonesia, Pakistan, Japan, Egypt. Experts believe that as much as three-fifths of the food required by the burgeoning populations of developing countries will come from irrigation.

Irrigation, however, is a temperamental ally. Diversions for irrigation can dry up an area downriver, as is happening with Russia's desiccated Aral Sea. Irrigation can cause waterlogging of the soil, salinization, subsidence. It can transport farm chemicals to groundwater, and mobilize toxic compounds that resided harmlessly in unirrigated soil.

In varying degrees, most of these problems now challenge California's Central Valley. Many who live and work there now realize they have taxed the environment to the limits and beyond. As a result, irrigation farming is in gradual transition to more sustainable agriculture.

To sense the lay of the land, I drove out of San Francisco toward Fresno, in the southern lobe of the valley. As I pushed southward, the highway acquired a slight downhill grade. Near Mendota I reached the bottom of an immense basin, where the land lies 30 feet lower than it did a hundred years ago. Here the pumping of groundwater for irrigation has caused the subsidence of an area the size of Connecticut. When downpours swell the San Joaquin River, Mendota and other subsidence towns routinely erect sandbag barricades to hold off the inevitable floodwaters.

Bustling Fresno sits above abundant groundwater; it is one of the largest American cities to draw its water entirely from underground sources. Years ago traces of DBCP, an agricultural pesticide, appeared in municipal water. The city closed down about a quarter of its wells, and moved to install charcoal filters. In 1977, California banned the chemical; a nationwide ban followed. Even so, DBCP remains the state's leading groundwater contaminant. Some wells have been cleaned up, but most large remediation plans are expensive, and people have largely lost interest.

Largely, but far from entirely. Farmer Paul Buxman of Dinuba remembers vividly when his two-year-old son contracted leukemia. Soon afterward Mr. Buxman discovered a high level of DBCP in his well water, and was told not to drink it or bathe in it. He recalled: "We had been mixing the formulas for our babies with this water." His son later recovered, but others did not. Elsewhere in the southern valley, a handful of towns have seen high levels of cancer in children. These "cancer clusters" have been charged to pesticides, but proof is lacking.

I consulted my San Joaquin soils map. Areas threatened by salinity were bounded by red lines. The lines embraced immense expanses along the floor of the valley—perhaps a fifth of all the irrigated land. I headed toward the place in Fresno where experts were paid to worry about such things—the Department of Agriculture's Water Management Research Laboratory on the edge of town.

"Scientists come here from all over the world to learn about coping with soil salinity," said agricultural engineer James E. Ayars. We studied a wall map studded with little tags marking the visitors' home countries. "Pakistanis, Chinese, Indians, Turks, Israelis—the Israelis practically live here. Salinity is a global problem. Perhaps a third of all irrigated land in the world is salt affected.

"All fresh water contains salts," said Dr. Ayars. "With proper irrigation they are not a problem. They build up in the soil when you over-irrigate. Salts also accumulate when you lack proper drains to carry them off. We're tackling both problems."

Another irrigation lesson—a bitter one—seared the valley environment like a branding iron. The lesson was learned at the ill-fated Kesterson Wildfowl Refuge. In the early 1980s, biologists with the Fish and Wildlife Service conducted a health check on fish and migratory birds inhabiting the 1,280-acre Kesterson Reservoir, centerpiece of the refuge. The reservoir, stopover for thousands of wintering waterfowl, was fed by drainage from irrigation on the west side of the San Joaquin Valley, at the foot of the Coast Range. The west-side ranches grew bumper crops. But when the Bureau of Reclamation built their irrigation system, two key elements had been omitted: a study of the soil's natural chemical content, and a drain line extending to San Francisco Bay. In lieu of this drain, the reservoir had become the catch basin for the irrigation drainage.

The biologists who made the check were uneasy—worried about soil chemicals, particularly selenium, that the drain water might be accumulating in the reservoir.

Their fears were well founded. Plants and animals contained enormous concentrations of selenium—often a hundred times normal. Eggs of ducks and other waterfowl held deformed embryos. Eggs that hatched often produced deformed young that soon died. Dead adult birds strewed the site. Realizing that the reservoir was a death trap, officials resorted to firing explosives to scare away wildfowl drawn to the tempting water. Kesterson became a symbol of ills that can flow from elaborate agricultural schemes that shortcut environmental safeguards.

"Part of the problem stemmed from that missing soil analysis," said Dr. James Biggar of the University of California at Davis, one of many irrigation scientists whose academic work focused on Kesterson. "The westside soils had washed down from the Coast Range, which once was an ancient seabed. Marine sediments are high in salts and trace elements. Area ranchers knew about the selenium because local plants take it up from the soil, and cattle eating the weeds go 'loco' with the blind staggers, a symptom of selenium toxicosis. When irrigation water arrived, it dissolved the selenium and mobilized it, and the drain water bore it down to Kesterson."

The revelation of Kesterson's selenium toxicosis, the first documented in the United States, stirred the Bureau of Reclamation to stop the use of the reservoir for irrigation drainage, and to plug the drains of westside irrigators. The Bureau drained the reservoir and brought in millions of tons of earth to cover its selenium-drenched floor. Kesterson was neutralized. Today surveys show no effects of selenium in Kesterson wildlife.

In the process of healing, Kesterson became a healer of the environment, a laboratory for studying what had gone wrong. With Dr. Biggar I toured the site, now largely an expanse of grasses and weeds—and alive with more wildlife than I had seen anywhere else in the valley.

A small part of the old reservoir, however, was different: The Bureau had not covered this part with clean earth, and the reservoir floor lay exposed. This part became the laboratory for learning how to handle toxics in soils.

Driving along Duck Club Road, we stopped at plots where Dr. Biggar and Dr. William Frankenburger of UC-Riverside were testing the removal of selenium by bioremediation—encouraging microbes to gasify the element and volatilize it harmlessly into the atmosphere. "The process is slow, but it's inexpensive and effective," said Dr. Biggar. "We calculate that in seven to ten years the microbes should remove enough selenium for the safe growing of crops."

We moved to a plot that explored another detoxicant. It looked weedy, unpromising. "These are selenium-tolerant plants that, like the microbes, take up the element and volatilize it. Broccoli, barley, and rice are especially good. We call it agroremediation. A farmer using plants to remove selenium on the west side of the valley can sell them as hay on the east side, where soils have a selenium deficiency. Animals require small amounts of selenium," said Dr. Biggar. "The most successful technique is the combined action of the plants and microbes—that's really fast."

Could a Kesterson happen elsewhere?

Definitely. "Farmers in other states are beginning to irrigate the same bad soils some Californians insist on farming," said Dr. Gary S. Banuelos of the Fresno Water Management Lab. "Toxic soil can sit there harmlessly until overirrigation sets the toxins in motion. We see this now in Colorado, Montana, the Dakotas, Wyoming, Utah—a dozen hot spots. The experimental work at Kesterson can help prevent another Kesterson."

*Pelicans flock to a nutrient-rich salt marsh in the Mississippi Delta. Here, where fresh water meets salt water, nature brews an ecosystem of incredible richness. More than 150 bird species and 200 kinds of fishes depend on the nation's wetlands, which support a third of the country's endangered and threatened plant and animal species. Near the U. S.*

*border with Mexico (opposite), man's hand lies heavy on this estuary of the Tijuana River—assaulted by sewage, trash, and street runoff.*

*FOLLOWING PAGES: Cabbage palmettos and saw grass in Everglades National Park call to mind the pristine wetlands that once covered most of southern Florida.*

We have altered the air. We have changed much of the land. What have we done to the oceans? This sloshing 70 percent of the planetary surface is perhaps the least tarnished of the three great spheres. But, like the proverbial ring around the bathtub, dark stains tarnish the margins of the ocean basins, where the marine environment laps shores besmirched by civilization. In addition, many of the creatures that dwell in the oceans are undergoing violent population swings as fishermen decimate the species we most like to eat, and other species take their places.

Compared to the productive soil, the sea yields a thin gruel for bowls on the world dinner table;

*Atlantic spotted dolphins chase the sunlight. Marine mammals—emblems of the oceans' glories and barometers of the oceans' health—today suffer from polluted habitats.*

acre for acre the ocean harvest equals only a fortieth of the land's. Yet the high protein content of the annual catch means survival for hundreds of millions of coastal people.

Each year the world's commercial fishermen bring into port about a hundred million tons of finfish and shellfish. Surprisingly, the catch rises slightly almost every year, as if there were no limit to the sea's powers of replenishment. But most experts believe the limits have been reached or perhaps exceeded. And in some heavily fished and polluted waters, fish populations have declined or collapsed.

Everyone who has baited a hook or cast a lure recalls a favorite fishing hole in lake or stream. So it is with fishermen on the broad seas; year after year they return to traditional oceanic fishing holes to fill their nets. Marine biologists, mapping these fishing grounds, have identified 49 rich and distinct ecosystems. Together they occupy a mere hundredth of the oceans, yet they produce 95 percent of the marine harvest. Known as Large Marine Ecosystems, or LMEs, they claim primary attention among those concerned with the environmental health of the ocean realm.

Two LMEs—the Black and the Baltic Seas—stand out as severely degraded, as does the Adriatic Sea within the Mediterranean Ecosystem. With each, a primary ailment is runoff of agricultural wastes, largely chemical fertilizers and livestock manure. These unwanted nutrients fertilize algae, which die and decay. In decaying, they deprive waters of oxygen, so that fishes die—the widespread problem known as eutrophication.

Worst off is the Black Sea, collecting basin for torrents of urban wastes and farm nutrients draining into the Danube River. "The nutrient load has modified the ecosystem of the Black Sea," said Dr. Kenneth Sherman of the Northeast Fisheries Science Center in Narragansett, Rhode Island. "Fish are being replaced by other species, primarily jellyfish. Similar conditions threaten the Baltic and the Adriatic Seas. Fortunately, there's hope of saving these."

Seven LMEs border U. S. coasts—the most for any nation. The Northeast Continental Shelf Ecosystem, reaching from Cape Hatteras to the Gulf of Maine, draws energy from cold, rich waters of the North Atlantic and from the Gulf Stream to rank as one of the world's most productive marine environments. It compares closely to the rich North Sea Ecosystem.

The Southeast Shelf Ecosystem, stretching from Hatteras to Florida's southern tip, derives its energy from nutrients deposited by numerous small estuaries, not unlike the East China Sea. The Gulf of Mexico is dominated by the output of the Mississippi River, and lacks a parallel elsewhere. Not so the California Current Ecosystem; its rich, upwelling waters support fish populations similar to those of Africa's Benguela Current and the mighty Peru Current, richest of all marine ecosystems. Valuable fisheries characterize the ecosystems of the Gulf of Alaska and the nearby East Bering Sea. Coral reefs surrounding the Hawaiian Islands support fish populations of the Insular Pacific Ecosystem.

Severe stress undermines several of the U. S. ecosystems. "The East

Coast and Gulf fisheries are in pretty sad shape," said Dr. William W. Fox, Jr., the National Oceanic and Atmospheric Administration's assistant administrator for fisheries; his revealing study of the mass drownings of dolphins in tuna fishing led to the design of remedial nets. "Commercial catches are half their potential, and economies are suffering. Pollution plays a small but growing role. The major contributors are habitat destruction through wetlands loss and just plain overfishing."

Overfishing was bludgeoning the Northeast ecosystem when I arrived at that depressed area. On Massachusetts' south shore, I hove into New Bedford, once the world whaling capital and long a busy fishing port. It was fishing weather—drizzly and calm—but scores of the old port's 400 boats lay moored at the piers, their captains discouraged by slim catches. I teamed up with Rodney Avila, a seasoned captain and fishery policy activist whose grandfather had emigrated from the Portuguese Azores to launch four generations of New Bedford fishermen.

"My grandfather was a conservationist. He taught my father and his six brothers to fish as he did—to take a variety of species so as not to deplete one, and to take only what you need. I teach the same to my two sons. A lot of fishermen think they own the fish out there. They don't. They are merely the vehicle for bringing them to the store, to the family table.

"What's happened to our fish? It's partly nature, partly us. We fish right off the Gulf Stream, and it has moved closer in recent decades; in the early 1960s the water temperature was in the 60s, and now it's in the 70s—too warm for good fishing. But the main problem is too many boats, too many fishermen. My solution is not very popular on the waterfront, but I say we need regulations—limits on fishing seasons and catches—a little sacrifice now so we and our children can continue to fish."

We toured the piers. Captain Avila's *Trident* was at sea; he had loaned it to the National Marine Fisheries Service to test a net with a special mesh permitting the escape of flatfish too small to keep. We admired a longline boat for swordfish, a scalloper with its dredges, and Captain Avila's second boat, *Seven Seas,* an otter trawl for flatfish. He paused approvingly at a plant that processed fish such as dogfish and skates—the predators that were joining humans in depleting Northeastern fish stocks.

# How the world catch fluctuates

"Some species can respond quickly to environmental change," explained Dr. Sherman. "As desirable fishes are depleted, the responsive species fill their niches, but almost always they are of a lower level of desirability. In many of the ecosystems these are members of the herring family—sardines and other Clupeids. Natural forces also alter the ecosystems. Recent shifts in currents off Japan and Chile have stimulated dramatic increases in commercial catches. Natural changes in temperature and salinity can also stress ecosystems and harm fisheries; this has been a factor in the depletion of cod stocks of the Newfoundland Shelf Ecosystem."

Compared to the overfished but relatively pristine open ocean, the coastal margins present a disheartening scene. We are defiling these priceless habitats badly. "About 75 percent of (Continued on page 130)

A galaxy of plankton draws an underwater camera in Mexico's Sea of Cortés. Made up of tiny plants and animals, plankton forms the core of the sea's rich food webs. Swarms of shrimp-like krill (above) feast on phytoplankton—plants— and in turn become food for squid and humpback whales (top).

FOLLOWING PAGES: Fishermen empty a cod trap off Newfoundland. Overfishing has cut deep into the millions of fish that once schooled off Canadian shores. A July 1992 ban on catching northern cod may be extended to the year 2000; to date, the ban has cost the fishing industry thousands of jobs.

*Crowded Virginia Beach mirrors a trend: Some 127 million people— more than half the U. S. population—soon will live within 50 miles of a coast. With humans come medical wastes and other pollution that degrade habitats for people and animals alike. Syringes turned up on New York's Coney Island. On Key Largo, Florida, plumes of pesticides kill mosquitoes but the chemicals filter into the water table and eventually reach the ocean. A fish stenciled by children in Eugene, Oregon, reminds people not to dump toxic materials into storm drains.*

Amid its 1,250 miles of bright grandeur, Australia's Great Barrier Reef shelters marine creatures that range from plankton to humpback whales. The reef, which began forming some 30 million years ago, is built of calcified skeletons of tiny animals known as coral polyps. In tropical waters worldwide, coral reefs create habitats for about one-fourth of all marine species. This rich diversity earns them the title "tropical rain forests of the ocean." Like rain forests, coral reefs rank among Earth's most endangered ecosystems. In the Florida Keys, a dying sea fan (opposite) is perhaps a victim of parasites or polluted water.

commercial fish and shellfish are dependent on inshore ecosystems for reproduction, growth, and migration," said William Fox. "In the Gulf of Mexico and the southeast Atlantic the dependence is above 90 percent. With almost all of these species, the catches are at or near historic low levels.

"Much of the decline is due to coastal habitat degradation—lost and damaged wetlands, toxic chemical releases, alteration of freshwater flows by dams and other diversions, and nutrient overenrichment from agricultural and sewage runoff. The greatest degradation occurs where coastal populations are greatest. Unfortunately, coastal counties are growing at four times the national average; by the year 2010 an estimated 54 percent of the U. S. population will live within 50 miles of a coast."

The crucial role of inshore waters in the health of the marine environment led Congress to order NOAA to establish an alliance known as the Coastal Zone Management Program. The 24 participating states and 5 territories share NOAA's substantial research into coastal ecologies. They also acquire significant regulatory authority, including the right, in some cases, to veto proposed federal uses of coastal land—a prized weapon.

From NOAA's James Burgess and William Millhouser, I learned of CZMP's efforts to stem coastal degradation: working for setback requirements; helping localities with wetland conservation, such as the effort of Charleston, South Carolina, to improve the harbor and build a beltway without damaging extensive marshes; encouraging states like Oregon, which is extending coastal protection well out to sea; protecting 22 estuarine reserves around the nation for environmental research and education.

NOAA also oversees marine sanctuaries, strung like a necklace along the coasts of the lower 48 states. "The sanctuaries," said Trudy Coxe, then director of the CZMP, "protect areas of unique value that are under escalating pressures of use."

Ms. Coxe had just returned from an inspection of newly designated Stellwagen Bank off Cape Cod, and her enthusiasm was volcanic. "We saw an 80-foot fin whale, the second largest mammal on Earth after the blue whale. A pod of at least 600 white-sided dolphins leaped in the wake of our vessel. The bank is a glacial sand moraine that harbors a large population of sand lances; they attract the porpoise and five species of whales that in turn attract a million tourists a year."

She extolled the other sanctuaries: Norfolk Canyon off Virginia; the site of the sunken Civil War ironclad *Monitor,* off Cape Hatteras; Gray's Reef off Georgia; the Florida Keys; Flower Garden Banks off Texas; California's Channel Islands; Monterey Bay; and North Puget Sound. Because it was winter when I found opportunity for a sanctuary visit, I opted for the southernmost, the sun-drenched arc of the Florida Keys.

The sanctuary's 2,800 square miles embrace an awesome resource: the world's third largest coral reef, after Australia's Great Barrier Reef and that off Belize in Central America. In shallow flats between thousands of mangrove-tufted keys sway two-thirds of all the world's sea-grass species. Exotic reef fish flash like gems among reclusive lobsters, four species of gliding turtles, and profusions of sponges.

Enter the annual influx of reef users and abusers: two million tourists; tens of thousands of pleasure boats that all too often drop anchors on the fragile corals; thousands of commercial fishermen dropping more anchors; a million lobster traps disturbing grasses and corals; treasure salvors spewing tailings; jet skiers plowing grasses; snorklers and scuba divers poking corals; drug traffickers running aground on the reef beside tankers and freighters and refugee boats; pollutants from sugarcane and cattle farms via the Everglades; pollutants from Tampa Bay; pollutants from Key West and Miami.

The February air was balmy, the water chill, when my friend John Lodmell and I donned snorkels and joined NOAA's Lt. (jg.) Richard Wingrove in the shallow chop near Looe Key. Three weeks earlier a sailboat had run aground; we swam over the smashed coral heads, many of them hundreds of years in the growing. Damage caused by earlier groundings furrowed nearby corals.

"Part of my work is responding to groundings," said Lieutenant Wingrove. "A lot of small craft have grounded lately, particularly on weekends. The cumulative damage from them is greater than from major vessels. The big ones tend to run aground to the north, where the Gulf Stream flows close to land and ships hug the shore. A freighter or tanker wipes out a coral area the size of a football field. We had so many large-ship groundings—three in one awful ten-day period—that now ships longer than 50 meters [164 feet] must stay out beyond the 600-foot depth."

We boated around wave-washed Looe Key, draped with the wreck of a grounded shrimper that had been loaded with drugs. Three boats carrying tourist divers bobbed at mooring buoys put out by sanctuary volunteers to dissuade crews from dropping anchors on the coral. Looking seaward, Lieutenant Wingrove ruefully eyed a southbound freighter. "She's well above the legal 50 meters and inside the depth limit, trying to avoid the Gulf Stream. But I can't send out my patrol team—the water's too rough for their safety."

We turned inland, into the sheltered domain of mangroves and seagrass flats, of legendary tarpon and bonefish and permit, of pollutants pouring in from Florida's teeming coasts and agricultural interior, of freshwater flows reduced by heavy diversions to the Miami area. "By every measure," said Lieutenant Wingrove, "the ecology is declining here: coral areas, water quality, fish catch…everything. I've watched it over the years."

# Controlling contaminants

"For a decade we've been monitoring the chemicals found in shellfish, fish, and bottom sediments at nearly 300 sites along the coasts," said Dr. Charles N. Ehler of NOAA, who initiated the monitoring. "As a general rule, the highest levels of contamination occur in the most urbanized coastal areas, particularly those with poor natural flushing like Boston Harbor and the Hudson River-Raritan Bay estuary. The main contaminants are trace metals, DDT, PCBs, and hydrocarbons from burning coal and oil.

"The nation has passed laws and spent hundreds of billions of dollars to control these, and in most cases the levels (Continued on page 136)

Trouble faces the Great Lakes basin, home to some 40 million Canadians and Americans. The Detroit River, flowing under clouds of steam from a steel plant that has spent 150 million dollars in recent years to reduce toxic emissions, carries sewage effluent from scores of nearby municipalities. Water fouled by such poisonous chemicals as dioxin, PCBs, and DDT has caused birth defects in birds and disease in fish like the bullhead (below), a native of Wisconsin's Fox River and a victim of lip cancer. There's only one way to save the abused ecosystem and protect human health, say environmentalists: Eliminate the pollution.

FOLLOWING PAGES: Creating a paradoxically beautiful abstract pattern, bubbles of compressed air cleanse industrial sludge in this aerial view of a waste-water purification lagoon along the Mississippi River near Baton Rouge, Louisiana.

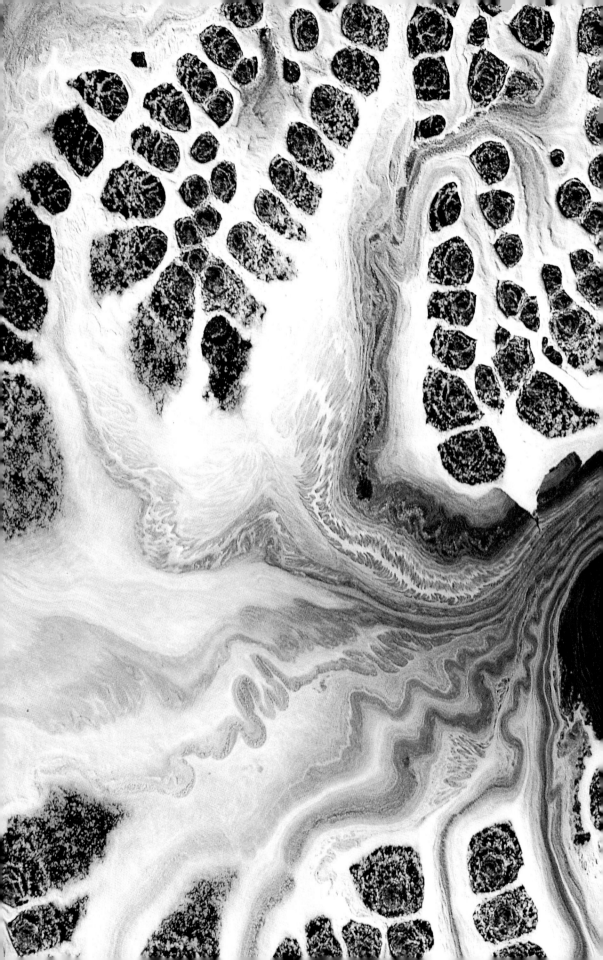

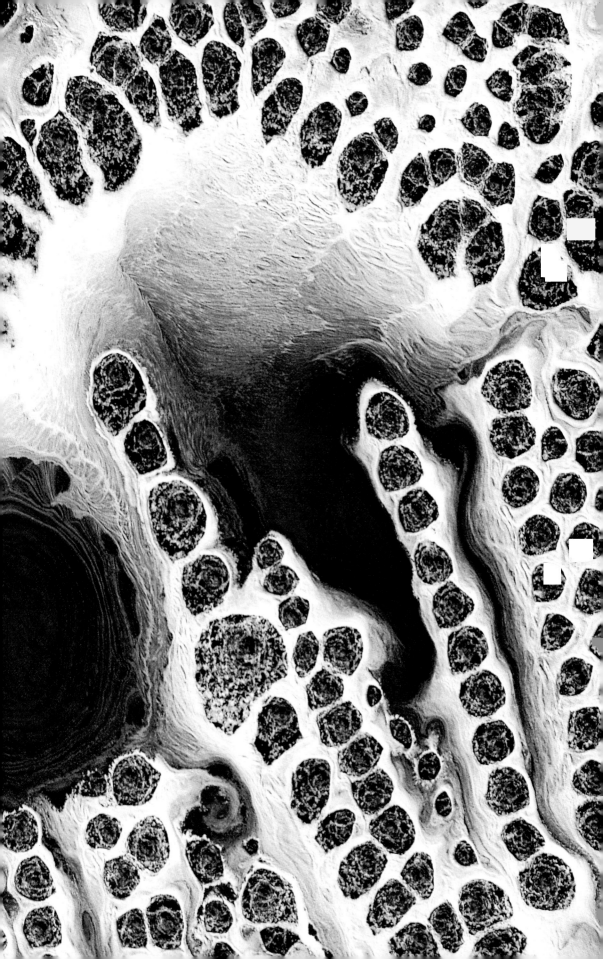

are dropping. Hot spots persist, such as DDT contamination off Los Angeles from an old manufacturing site. In such a case we determine the extent and value of damage to the natural resources and then recover against the responsible party, just as Exxon had to pay for the oil spill in Alaska."

When the *Exxon Valdez* shuddered onto the rock of Prince William Sound in 1989, Native Americans living along that tainted coast faced a crisis: Were the fish on which they subsisted safe to eat? Within days a NOAA task force screened the content of food fish for 13 Alaskan villages. The results showed that the fish had indeed taken in toxic oil hydrocarbons, but had metabolized and excreted the toxic elements in their bile: The flesh was safe to eat. The same tests showed that mussels, lacking comparable digestive tracts, in some cases retained the toxins in their flesh.

The task force and its monitoring technology sprang from NOAA's Environmental Conservation Division in Seattle, directed by Dr. Usha Varanasi. "We look for effects not only of persistent pollutants such as DDT and PCBs," she said," but transitory chemicals that could do damage and then disappear. If we monitor only the effects of the long-lasting chemicals, we can control them and wonder why degradation is continuing.

"The thousands of chemicals that satisfy society's technological and economic needs are finding their way into the marine environment. Of particular concern are the fossil-fuel hydrocarbons emitted by our chimneys and car exhausts. Most of the contaminants settle to the bottom. Fish that feed on bottom-dwelling organisms are showing the effects—in DNA changes that lead to the formation of cancerous tumors, in immune-system failure, and in impairment of growth and reproduction.

"The goal," continued Dr. Varanasi, "is to identify the levels of contamination that are harmful to the ecosystem, and the levels we can live with. I like to compare the integrity of an ecosystem to that of a clay vessel. If a part of the vessel's lip is chipped away, the vessel still functions. If a chip is removed from the bottom, the usefulness of the vessel is destroyed. Similarly, not every part of an ecosystem is essential. But we have to know which parts are which."

Fortunately for waste-strewing humans, estuaries are durable ecosystems, able to withstand wide fluctuations in their conditions. Witness ailing Chesapeake Bay, the largest U.S. estuary, and scene of the nation's largest environmental repair effort. Until recently, the state of the Chesapeake saddened the spirit, and its fate still hangs in the balance.

At its nadir in 1985 it had lost 96 percent of its once abundant hickory shad, 70 percent of its noble striped bass, two in three of the American shad prized by George Washington, 90 percent of its cherished oysters. Half the bay's wetlands had been destroyed, 40 percent of its embracing forests cut. Nutrients flowing in from overfertilized farms and lawns and detergents had nurtured explosions of algae that shaded bottom grasses, destroying 90 percent of this prime nursery habitat. Each year the storm drains of Baltimore, Washington, D.C., Richmond, and other watershed cities washed more oil into the bay than was spilled by the *Exxon Valdez*.

Yet the pristine Chesapeake was a natural paradise. Bay chronicler

Tom Horton described its seductions: "You will be hard-pressed to find another [bay] where the water twines more extensively with the land in dozens of rivers and thousands of creeks; where the depths are as moderate, the tides as minimal, the seas as kindly,...the seafood as abundant; where these and a dozen other factors, such as proximity to the nation's capital, conspire half so well to create water so eminently usable for so many purposes by such a large and growing population."

# When the dams came

Much that harmed the bay happened long ago. It happened, among other places, along the 46 major rivers whose waters welcomed the spawning runs of bay fishes. "As far back as colonial times, laws forbade the blocking of fish spawning runs," explained Jay O'Dell of the Maryland Department of Natural Resources. "People salted down shad by the barrel, and caught them and river herring for fertilizer, just as the Indians did. But the laws were ignored. Dams rose for water power to run mills and for reservoirs. Most economically important bay species are anadromous—they have to ascend streams from the ocean to spawn in fresh water. The blockages meant disaster, not only for the bay but for the coastal Atlantic Ocean for which the bay is a nursery.

"Here is your typical problem," said Mr. O'Dell, pointing to an eight-foot-high dam over which poured waters of the Little Patuxent River. "The dam backs up water for the Army's Fort Meade and the National Security Agency. It totally blocked thousands of shad and herring that ascended each spring, many as far as the fall line at Savage.

"Here's what the DNR did about it." At the west end of the dam we looked down on a fish ladder, obviously much newer than the dam itself. River water plunged down a staircase of wooden baffles, took a right-angle turn, and descended until it merged with the main flow below the dam. The fishway went into operation for the spring run of 1991—one of six at blockages along bay tributaries. Many more are planned. This kind of work is taking off across the country. New England and the Pacific Northwest have particularly vigorous fish passage programs.

Fortunately for Chesapeake Bay, in the 1970s the farsighted Mr. O'Dell launched a 16-year survey of the health of bay tributaries. He recalled: "Using a little flat-bottom boat, I mapped every tributary as far upstream as I could navigate. Where I was stopped, I flagged a tree at the blockage, then came back in winter when visibility was better to survey upstream to the fall line or to a dam too high for a fishway. The study verified more than a thousand blockages, largely dams and highway culverts.

"Now the DNR is installing fishways as fast as it can get the money. In addition to federal, state, and private sources, some funding comes from environmental mitigation negotiations. If a developer or public facility destroys, say, a wetland, and cannot create another in the same watershed, it must pay the estimated value of the lost resource—money sometimes available for passages."

Though blocked for bay fish, the rivers are all too efficient as introducers of unwanted nutrients.

"The bay drains an enormous area—64,000 square miles," said Ann Powers at the office of the Chesapeake Bay Foundation in Annapolis, Maryland. "The large land-to-water ratio means that it receives a heavy load of effluents. The bay has a relatively narrow mouth and flushes poorly, causing pollutants to settle into the bottom sediments. The natural filters of wetlands and forests have suffered. The Eastern Shore has been scraped bare for farming, and the west side is a concrete crescent of development. With the filters diminished, rains wash pollutants directly into the bay."

Down a hallway, CBF ecologist Dr. Michael Hirshfield was grappling with one of the thorniest problems, agricultural runoff.

"I work with authorities and farmers in drainage-area states to adopt a philosophy of controlled nutrient applications: put on enough to nourish their crops and *no more*. Prevention of runoff is far cheaper than cleaning up after it. Animal wastes are the worst problem. Maryland, Pennsylvania, Virginia, New York—these are dairy states. The Delmarva Peninsula produces half a billion chickens a year. Hogs are a growing problem.

"Another approach is to encourage the development of filter strips to intercept nutrient-laden runoff. Buffers of grasses and trees along streams could check the escape of much nonpoint pollution."

Stubborn and insidious, nonpoint pollution is the nemesis of coastal waters. We already largely control "point" pollution—the wastes of cities and industries that flow manageably from a pipe. Nonpoint pollutants

*Oil spills exact huge tolls in cleanup and wildlife rescue, but oil-eating microbes helped avert disaster in 1990 in Galveston Bay (opposite),* *when they gobbled up spilled heavy oil. In Alaska, a worker tends to a harbor seal pup, a victim of the* Exxon Valdez *spill in 1989.*

wash into streams from diffuse sources, largely with runoff water from storms. In addition to farm wastes, they include soil eroded from fields and construction sites; the abundant urban detritus of street litter, pet waste, road salt, sand, and oil; and airborne chemicals from autos and smokestacks that fall with every rain. Nonpoint pollution defies remediation primarily because the source is each and every one of us. Controlling it could impinge on lifestyles and affect future land use and development—the Achilles heel of the coastal environment.

"Most developers are blind to their effects on coastal waters," said Dr. John B. Pearce of the Northeast Fisheries Science Center. "To control the health of the sea, we must monitor what takes place on the land, where so many problems originate." Added NOAA's Dr. Ehler: "If we can't manage the movement of people to the coasts, especially in the South and Southwest where it's worst, the additional pollution from new sources will overwhelm progress we've already made." Yet projections see the population of just the Maryland, Virginia, and Pennsylvania portions of the Chesapeake drainage area rising from today's 13 million to 16 million by the year 2020.

Despite the pressure, there is some progress, and this gives heart to those who nurture the treasured estuary. "The sea grasses are returning to parts of the bay. That's an indicator of reviving health," said CBF's Dr. Hirshfield. "Phosphate discharges are down dramatically, and nitrogen is at least holding steady." Draconian fishing controls have contributed to recoveries of striped bass and American shad, and yellow perch are coming back in areas where they were once considered endangered or lost. Some authorities believe that the declines may be arrested—a corner turned.

T he type of habitat destruction that plagues the bay is wreaking similar environmental damage on the continent's Pacific Coast, in the immense realm of the Pacific salmon. Here, sweeping alterations of the land and competing demands on river water threaten one of the most lavish and inspiring endowments of living creatures to grace the planet.

The salmon species of the Pacific Coast win renown, of course, for their epic migrations—rhythmic journeys up rapids and falls as far as 900 miles. They excavate their redds in bottom gravels, spawn, and die long before their descendants hatch. In the Columbia Basin alone, before the white man arrived, an estimated 16 million chinooks, pinks, chums, cohos, and sockeyes annually brought the bounty of the sea to tribes of Indians fishing the riverbanks, and to the bear and eagle and mountain lion. Large populations of steelheads swelled this largesse, as did sea-run cutthroat trout.

Today a mere two and a half million salmon enter those rivers each year, despite annual releases of nearly 200 million fry by regional hatcheries. In northern California the runs are even more reduced. Alaska populations fluctuate but show the least decline. An immense sport fishery is threatened, and so is a gallant embodiment of Western culture and spirit.

Because of the attrition, salmon in both the Northwest and in California are entering the lists of endangered and threatened species, and many already are believed extinct. How can animals that still number in the millions be so listed? The answer lies in the salmon's peculiar homing instinct—its legendary urge to return, after years in the ocean, to spawn in its native stream. The fish of each watershed constitute a recognizable stock, or race, genetically imprinted with the chemistry of that stream. If a stream is blocked, and the stock dies out, none will replace it. Thus a stock can be threatened, be endangered, or become extinct even though the species itself survives in large numbers.

Fifty years ago the American Fisheries Society identified some 400 stocks in the Columbia River and its major tributary, the Snake. Today, of 214 studied stocks, it reports that many face the risk of extinction. A look at Snake River sockeyes tells the story. Once, hundreds of thousands breasted the rapids. By 1991 diversion dams stopped all but four sockeyes— three males and a female—from reaching their last Idaho refuge, Redfish Lake. When I visited the Northwest a year later, a single sockeye, a male, had reached Redfish. Its sperm had been frozen in hope that females might arrive the next year. For all practical purposes that stock, too, was extinct.

## The mightiest of salmon

Formerly, in California, a million chinooks—the largest salmon species—ascended the Sacramento and San Joaquin Rivers. In 1990, Sacramento River winter-run chinooks became the first salmon to be listed as threatened under the Endangered Species Act. Soon the state was holding survivors in saltwater tanks as insurance against extinction.

San Joaquin chinooks fared worse. "Because the San Joaquin drains the High Sierra, a huge chinook run went up in spring," said Dr. Peter Moyle of the University of California at Davis. "They holed up all summer in deep mountain pools. For the Indians, it was like having a freezer full of 15-pound fish, ready to spear. Then the Bureau of Reclamation built the Friant Dam— with no fishway. The spring chinooks became extinct.

"Many human activities combine to destroy salmon habitat, or deny access to it," continued Dr. Moyle, whose documentation of spring chinook declines was made by snorkeling among his subjects. "Mining and grazing encourage erosion. Logging causes erosion and removes shade, causing water temperatures to rise beyond fish tolerance. Industry pollutes. Flood control and navigation projects raise barriers to migration. Cities divert water. Worst are the water diversions for irrigation. Then comes a drought, such as recently hit the West. The fish haven't a chance."

In all of salmondom, the busiest thoroughfare for migration traditionally was the Columbia-Snake system. Today 59 major dams and 195 lesser barriers transform the rivers into a staircase of lakes. They bring immense benefits to people: hydropower that is clean and cheap, barge traffic deep into the western interior, flood control, water for agriculture and industry, and recreational boating and fishing.

Surprisingly, the primary problem of these dams lies not in the adult salmon's grueling journey upriver to spawn, but in the juveniles' trip downriver to the sea. I took a briefing on salmon behavior at Bonneville Dam, the first titanic riser of the long stairway of Columbia dams.

Guided by their mysterious homing instinct, sockeye salmon (below) swim up the Adams River toward spawning beds in British Columbia. In contrast to Canada's usually heavy salmon return, tallies by fish counters, like Pat Jones at Washington's Bonneville Dam (opposite), show that the United States fares poorly—67 stocks of Columbia River salmon have vanished, and some 50 others are at risk. Among the causes of salmon decline are power dams and overfishing, as well as habitat degradation from agricultural runoff and sedimentation of spawning streams caused by logging and grazing. A young

salmon's life cycle leads from river to sea and back. Dam reservoirs often slow their passage, dooming their biological adaptation to the salt water ahead. To help young salmon mature in Pacific feeding grounds, a barge carries wild fish seaward, through locks and safely past Columbia River dams.

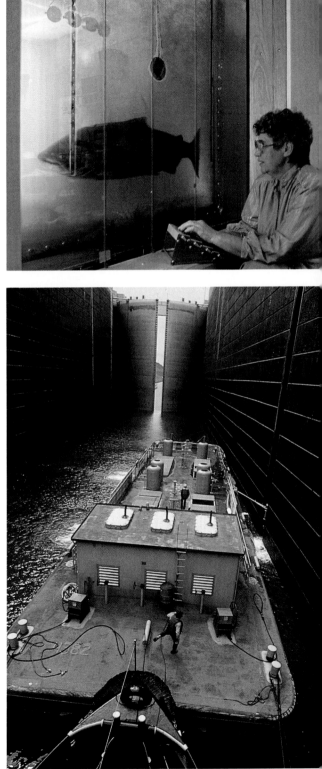

"We can get fish upriver. Tagging shows that on average only 3 to 4 percent of those passing a dam fail to pass the next dam," said Gary Johnson, fish biologist for the U. S. Army Corps of Engineers, which built and operates many of the major dams. "Most salmon stocks evolved so the juveniles would be swimming downriver in spring, riding the natural freshet of snowmelt. Now that dams pool the water, there are no freshets to carry the young fish. They are becalmed. Because they are maturing as they migrate, many revert to a freshwater phase and stop migrating, while others enter the ocean less fit than they should be for saltwater survival."

Those spinning hydroelectric turbines—don't their gnashing blades grind up descending juveniles like meat in a blender?

"The National Marine Fisheries Service spent four years studying that here at Bonneville," said Mr. Johnson. "They monitored the passage of two million marked salmon. The mortality rate of juveniles passing through the turbines was 2 to 4 percent. After all, the turbines turn at only about a revolution a second, and the blade tips pass so close to the turbine walls that few fish are injured. Fish descending by channels *around* the turbines suffered much greater losses, partly because predatory squawfish were waiting below. The Bonneville administration now offers a three-dollar bounty on squawfish—bounty fishing supports a small industry."

When drought conspires with the many water diversions to hobble juveniles in their downriver run, the Corps of Engineers mobilizes barges and trucks to transport fish—many from hatcheries—around the

*Inside a fish ladder on Maryland's Patapsco River, author Tom Canby (left) and Maryland naturalist Jay O'Dell inspect shad before sending them on up the passageway. Shad live in salt water, but every spring they ascend rivers to spawn. Dams and other blockages in the Chesapeake Bay area impeded migration, and shad, herring, and other anadromous populations declined severely. Bay programs are now reopening historic spawning habitats by removing some obstructions and installing ladders to channel fish around others.*

dams for release below Bonneville. This cumbersome measure flies in the face of a growing belief that hatchery fish are part of the problem—that these pampered progeny lack the genetic toughness to survive in river and sea, and are diluting the genetic strength of wild fish.

Ultimately, most authorities agree, a decision must be made about releasing water to provide the flow needed to flush the young salmon down to sea. Precedent for this came in the California chinook crisis, in which a court acting under the Endangered Species Act directed that water normally used for irrigation and hydropower be given to the fish during spawning.

Salmon country embraces virtually all of the great temperate rain forest—the home of the old-growth monarchs and the spotted owl and the ailing timber industry. Forestry practices doubtless will feature large in the protection of salmon ecosystems.

Yet I saw none of the polarization that darkened the issue of old-growth timbering and the spotted owl. Observed writer John Balzar, "No one here wears T-shirts mocking the salmon the way they do the owl." The National Marine Fisheries Commission has appointed a recovery team, largely from universities in the region, to draft a salmon strategy.

Some believe the salmon issue could change the direction of environmental stewardship. "It could make the owl look trivial," said Dr. Arthur McKee of Oregon State University. "Salmon affect everything—timber, power generation, agriculture, offshore fishing, Native Americans—everything. The issue will dominate the land use of the Pacific Northwest."

*Contaminated waters damage a shellfish growing area near Sandy Hook, New Jersey. Pollution from two major sources, sewage treatment plants and urban runoff, led to this warning—grim evidence of a burgeoning coastal population.*

*FOLLOWING PAGES: A lined sea horse, a young blue crab, and red seaweed benefit from a watershed-wide campaign to clean up Chesapeake Bay. The return of sea grasses in parts of the bay promises renewed health for this threatened estuary.*

From the remotest corners of the planet, nondescript white bags flow constantly to a squat brick building in Frederick, Maryland. The bags' contents appear worthless—blossoms and leaves, bits of bark, twigs, and wood, algae, seaweed, sponges.

Most of the contents *are* worthless. Some are treasures beyond value.

The brick building belongs to the National Cancer Institute, the United States' premiere health agency for fighting cancer and AIDS. The bags hold samples of plants and animals whose good health in the wild showed that they might possess protective chemicals against disease or insect pests. These natural chemicals could arm human

*Threatened hunter, a jaguar finds a quiet moment in Belize. The destruction of tropical rain forest— one of the jaguar's habitats—poses severe threats to biological diversity.*

beings against those two great enemies of human life and welfare.

NCI's search for natural cures to cancer and AIDS is a race against time. Many potentially curative plants grow in tropical rain forests. Many of these plant species exist only in tiny microenvironments, and in minuscule numbers, part of the rain forests' legendary biodiversity. With rain forests under assault by loggers, colonists, cattle growers, and fuelwood gatherers, priceless curative plants are disappearing before fire, machete, chainsaw, and bulldozer, often overnight.

Hear a typical horror story:

"We were collecting samples in the rain forest on Luzon in the Philippines," recalled Dr. Doel Soejarto, of the University of Illinois at Chicago. "I gathered material from a tree of the genus *Neouvaria* and shipped it to our labs in Chicago. Screening showed activity against cancer. My colleagues asked me to collect more. I returned to the site. It had become a cornfield. I combed the surrounding forest, and made two more trips, searching, searching, searching, in vain.

"By chance another scientist found a *Neouvaria* on the Philippine island of Samar. I went to that site. By then the tree was a stump, probably cut for firewood. After two days of searching I found two more large trees, and sent samples back to Chicago. Screening again showed that the plant is, indeed, active against cancer in vitro. Further studies of the compound isolated from the plant are being made."

## A trio of grave concerns

When authorities rank threats to the environment, most head their list with global warming, ozone depletion, and the threat to biodiversity. The first two problems are reversible—global warming and ozone loss can be halted, even forced into retreat. Not so with biodiversity.

The National Science Foundation, not noted for exaggeration, calls the problem a "crisis." Unless the trend can be reversed, noted a milestone NSF report, "the rate of extinction over the next few decades…will ultimately result in the loss of a quarter or more of the species on earth."

One of the signatories to the report was Dr. Edward O. Wilson of Harvard University, probably the world's most respected authority on biological diversity. In an address before the National Geographic Society, Wilson spoke of five great past extinctions, wrought by asteroid impacts and global climate change. He continued:

"Virtually all students of the extinction process agree that biological diversity is in the midst of its sixth great crisis, this time precipitated entirely by man.… We have become the greatest catastrophic agent since the extinction spasm that closed the Mesozoic era 65 million years ago."

Plant and animal species abound most profusely in the humid tropics, where pressures of the exploding human population are also greatest: Indonesia, Malaysia, and the Philippines in Asia; Cameroon, Gabon, and Uganda in Africa. The heartland of the planet's diversity lies in the Andean nations of Ecuador, Colombia, and Peru. Each stands with a foot in Amazonia, combining its species wealth with that of the myriad ecosystems that stairstep the mighty Andes as they rise from steamy jungle to perennial glaciers 20,000 feet high: coastal forests, dry forests, cloud forests, deserts, inter-Andean valleys, bleak plateaus known as *páramos.*

The heart of biodiversity's heartland throbs in Ecuador. Acre for acre, this equatorial, Colorado-size ark nurtures more kinds of living organisms than any other country on Earth. Scientists studying a half-mile-square area of the Río Palenque Biological Station in Ecuador's coastal forest counted 1,033 plant species, some known only from a single living specimen. By comparison, the entire United States contains only some 20,000 different plants.

To bring the problems of biodiversity into focus, conservationist Norman Myers identified areas combining richest diversity and highest risk to habitat. This work permitted Conservation International to select 15 priority areas for attention: the coastal forest of Ecuador and Colombia, Brazil's Atlantic forest, Madagascar, Indonesia, the Philippines, Central American forests, Andean slopes, forests of upper Guinea, the Eastern Arc Mountains in Tanzania, India's Western Ghats, Sinharaja Forest in Sri Lanka, the eastern Himalaya, peninsular Malaysia, northern Borneo, and Melanesia.

Because no alarm bell sounds when an extinction takes place, and because there is no complete inventory of Earth's life-forms, scientists freely admit they can only guess at the number of species being lost. That woefully incomplete global inventory includes approximately 1.4 million species that are properly identified and classified as prescribed by the 18th-century Swedish naturalist, Carolus Linnaeus. Experts agree this is a mere fraction of the total. What is that total? Dr. Wilson estimates that a complete passenger list of the great Earth ark would include anywhere from 5 million to 80 million species.

Those unidentified species will not all be ho-hum bugs and mosses, if recent experience teaches. Two years ago scientists with the World Wildlife Fund, exploring a remote nature reserve in Vietnam, found a new large mammal species—a forest goat. Brazil has recently yielded two new monkeys—a tamarin and the cuddly, rat-size Maues marmoset. Entire new ecological frontiers have come to light—the strange ecosystems of mid-ocean volcanic vents, with their sulfur-eating bacteria and giant tube worms, and the rich ecosystem of the rain forest canopy, the exploration of which caused a dramatic upward revision of the estimated number of insect species. The next new world of biodiversity could be found in the deep oceans, where knowledge of the biota is skimpiest.

Though our knowledge of biodiversity suffers gaps and disagreements, there is little argument over key points:

The main cause of species loss is habitat loss.

At least half of the world's species inhabit the hard-pressed tropical forests, which cover only 7 percent of the landmass.

Wetlands provide another rich biological haven, and are similarly vulnerable to destruction. They constitute only about 5 percent of U. S. land,

*FOLLOWING PAGES: Painted faces can't mask the amusement of girls in Papua New Guinea with their first Polaroid picture. Outside intrusion endangers the world's cultural as well as biological diversity.*

*Along with produce, fish, clothing, and crafts, sellers at the Ver-o-Peso market in Belém, Brazil, offer a profusion of medicines from the rain forest. Teeming with wild plants, Amazonia is the world's greatest natural pharmacopeia, from which Indians gather leaves, bark, sap, stems, and roots to use in salves and infusions effective against ailments ranging from colds and fevers to skin infections and snakebites.*

yet are essential to nearly 35 percent of all U. S. rare and endangered species.

Every species represents a unique and potentially valuable collection of chemicals, as expressed in its genetic makeup.

This diversity—in plants, animals, fungi, and microorganisms—provides the basis for human health and prosperity.

And so it is with medicines. Some 7,000 of the chemical compounds used in drugs around the world come from natural products; they provide American druggists with 40 percent of the chemicals they use in filling prescriptions. Aspirin, the pill of choice everywhere, derives from a flowering plant, meadowsweet. The heart drug digitalis comes from a garden favorite, foxglove. The Madagascar rosy periwinkle produces two cancer-fighting chemicals that cure victims of once lethal Hodgkin's disease and a leukemia afflicting children. On and on.

The greatest natural pharmacopeia is the vast rain forest of Amazonia, home to a quarter of the world's 220,000 species of flowering plants—nature's most useful botanical chemists. For millions of generations, flowering plants have evolved chemical defenses against predators, defenses that make them toxic or repellent to animals that would eat them. Some of these chemicals possess the ability to kill unwanted cells, such as those in humans that multiply out of control as cancerous tumors. Others defend cells against enemies, such as bacteria, fungi, and insidious viruses—possibly including the HIV virus of AIDS.

For centuries Amazonia's pharmaceutical profusion has flowed downriver with other forest products to the city of Belém, at the mouth of the Amazon. It helps stock the crowded stalls of the famous Ver-o-Peso market on the riverbank, a vast and pungent display case for the natural wealth of Brazil's interior.

The Ver-o-Peso is a druggist's delight. Pharmacologist Elaine Elisabetsky of Brazil's University of Pará counted some 80 booths selling medicinal plants and potions. She found the vendors knowledgeable in prescribing remedies for symptoms their customers described. On a hot and humid Sunday, I too prowled those exotic booths, struggling to translate labels on bottles and bags written in Portuguese. I deciphered one that held a clear yellow fluid. *"Amor e Emprêgo,"* it said—"Love and Employment."

In the race to locate cures in vanishing plants, ethnobotanists turn to those who know forest medicines best, the native healers. This quest bears a dual urgency. Like many of their medicinal plants, the medicine men themselves, and their unique knowledge, stand at the brink of extinction.

"The shamans are a dying breed," said Dr. Mark J. Plotkin, an

Humans pin their hopes for better health on nature. The bark of the Pacific yew tree (left) contains taxol, a compound used in treating ovarian and breast cancer. Many folk remedies feature curative flora. A leaf from the "headache plant" soothes a Nigerian's aching forehead. In Siberut, Indonesia, the tattooed hands of a Mentawi shaman wrap a medicinal plant in another leaf to protect it. Few of the world's millions of species have been analyzed by scientists; folk healing often has identified those useful in producing new drugs. Every day, development destroys ecological niches, forever wiping out plant species that perhaps held the promise of miracle cures.

ethnobotanist with Conservation International. "The next generation isn't interested in their knowledge; they'd rather get pills from the missionaries. Each time a medicine man dies, it's as if a library has burned down."

Mark Plotkin spent portions of ten years with the Tirió Indians of Suriname in northeast Amazonia, one of the world's least disturbed areas of rain forest. He learned the Tirió language, drank their cassava beer fermented with saliva, and cataloged more than 200 plant species that cure earaches, ease childbirth, heal infections, soothe burns.

## Rescuing wisdom

Old age depleted the Tirió shaman ranks during Dr. Plotkin's period with them. "Then the missionaries moved away," he recalled, "and their modern medicine went with them. Meanwhile, the tribe had lost the knowledge of many of its native cures. I worked with the tribal leaders to choose four young, literate Indians to study my accounts of their medical lore, to relearn what they had lost. I call them the shaman's apprentices."

Today at Conservation International, Dr. Plotkin directs a Shaman's Apprentice Program that promotes continuity of tribal medical lore in Costa Rica and Suriname, and plans to expand to Colombia and New Guinea.

Partly with an eye toward possible medical discoveries, Costa Rica has pioneered a new approach to inventorying and marketing its rich biodiversity. The goal is formidable: to classify flora and fauna that could approach half a million species, so biological chemicals can be controlled and exploited as other nations control petroleum and minerals. An agreement stipulates that Costa Rica will provide medical samples to Merck & Co., Inc., the world's largest pharmaceutical organization, in return for a million-dollar payment and royalties on resulting sales. The arrangement could set a precedent for other tropical nations that fear the exploitation of their biological resources without fair payment by those who develop them.

The importance of biodiversity includes its role in a vital phenomenon known as interdependence. Amazonia's economically important Brazil nut provides an example. Though the trees are massive and the fruits tough, the mighty *castanha-do-pará* is vulnerable.

The tree cannot exist without five species of large-bodied bees; only they have the strength to pry open and pollinate the Brazil nut flower. When the mature fruits fall to the ground, rodents, particularly agoutis and squirrels—which are able to gnaw through the fruit's thick, woody walls—eat the fruit and carry off seeds to a cache, where the seeds may germinate. Each element is indispensable in the tree's web of life.

Because rain forests nurture the greatest wealth of biodiversity, special concern focuses on the deforestation of Amazonia. In Brazil a law limits cutting to 50 percent of a tract. The remnant stands, known as forest fragments, possess special importance for biodiversity. They are the residual sanctuaries for forest plants and animals. How hospitable are they to the forest survivors? Is a fragment of one size more friendly than other sizes? The answers could be crucial to species survival, for while cutting might be unstoppable, nations might at least tailor the surviving fragments for nature's benefit.

More than a decade ago Dr. Thomas E. Lovejoy, then with World Wildlife Fund and now an assistant secretary of the Smithsonian Institution, resolved to answer those questions. He and H.O.R. Schubart of Brazil's Institute for Amazonian Research located an area north of Manaus that was to be cleared for cattle fazendas. They arranged with the *patrons* that the clearing process leave fragments of different sizes—one hectare (about two and a half acres), ten hectares, and a hundred hectares—at locations the scientists had identified as desirable for research. At every prospective fragment, before cutting began, they conducted a detailed survey of the natural flora and fauna. Every type of tree, every species of certain groups of animals. Only this would permit precise measurements of deforestation's later effects, and provide a basis for wise governmental controls for protecting biodiversity.

The rainy season was beginning when my wife, Susan, and I left Manaus with avian ecologist Philip Stouffer and lurched northward on rutted BR-174, the link with the fragments-study area and distant Venezuéla. Fazendas known as *sitios*—weekend ranches of well-heeled citizens of Manaus—notched the largely undisturbed rain forest sweeping to each side of us for hundreds of miles.

"I work with fragments surrounded by pastures that have been abandoned to secondary forest growth," said Dr. Stouffer, as our four-wheel drive skidded along a rain-wet fazenda road toward base camp. "By netting birds and counting them, I determine the rate of repopulation. We find that when a fragment is first isolated, the birds largely vanish. Perhaps they move to the nearest undisturbed forest. As the second growth gets taller, the same kinds of birds that originally inhabited the fragment gradually return, though usually not in the same numbers. The larger the fragment, the greater the rate of return.

"I also look at the health of the birds that do return. Are they stressed by environmental changes in the fragment? I net them and study their feathers, which show bands of daily growth, something like tree rings. The bands of stressed birds will be closer. My results are extremely tentative, but they indicate that life for fragment birds is stressful."

We set forth on foot across recently cut and burned pasture to a one-hectare fragment. Where hundreds of stately trees should have stood, only a few dozen remained, clustered in the center. Root balls of fallen trees raised mounds on the forest floor. "When the surrounding forest is removed," said Dr. Stouffer, "wind drives in and topples trees, especially at the fragment edges. Sunlight reaches the forest floor at the edges, and dense vegetation springs up. Temperatures change throughout a fragment, and it becomes drier. It loses many animal species, including birds."

Thunder rumbled to the north as we crossed another pasture to a ten-hectare fragment. We penetrated the dense edge, then entered the reduced light of high-canopy forest. Dr. Stouffer stooped and picked up a tiny leaf-litter frog. A pair of red-and-green macaws alighted in a high tree and squawked restlessly. In this fragment, too, the wind had reached in and felled trees, though proportionately fewer than in the smaller remnant.

"Four species of monkeys still inhabit this tract," said Dr. Stouffer.

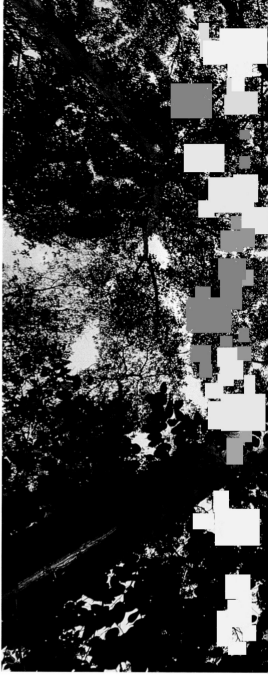

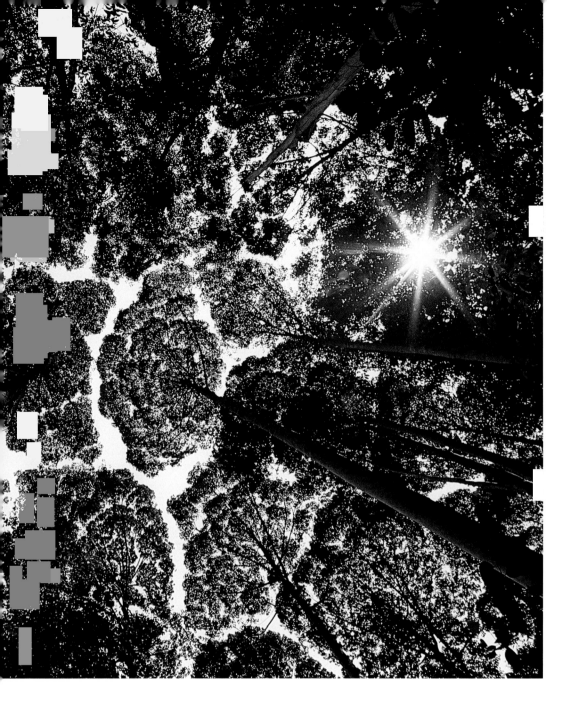

Life abounds most profusely in tropical forests, home of at least half the world's plant and animal species. The pinnacle of the lush realm is the rain forest canopy, a domain of branches, vines, and leaves some 150 feet above the forest floor. Between the tree crowns, fringes of daylight cut a pattern against the sky (above). Known as canopy "shyness," these gaps of polite distance may result from branches rubbing together or robbing each other of sunlight. Habitats exist from canopy to forest floor for animals and plants: Brazil's Toco toucan (opposite, top); Madagascar's rosy periwinkle, the source of a leukemia-fighting drug; Brazil's wild ginger, which attracts the ecosystem's most populous insect group, the ants; and Suriname's blue poison dart frog.

He pointed out an armadillo path, then scanned the treetops. "There are sloths here, but they're so slow and so high you seldom see them. In a normal forest you see army ants on the march, with birds swarming above, eating insects that try to get out of the ants' path. You don't see that in well-isolated ten-hectare fragments, because the ant-following birds don't stay in fragments that small unless they can also forage in tall secondary growth outside the fragment. We lack 10 of the 13 species of understory birds that travel as mixed-species flocks, and 10 of the 15 or so solitary species."

That night howler monkeys shattered the forest stillness as we accustomed ourselves to sleeping in hammocks. At dawn, songs poured from the forest. Holding out a microphone, Dr. Stouffer caught the call of a nearby fasciated antshrike. He played it back, and the bird popped into view, grasshopper in its beak, and searched with fiery red eyes for the "rival" whose call it had heard. A black-eared fairy hummingbird hovered hesitantly above me, perhaps drawn by my yellow shirt.

We crossed a stump-strewn pasture toward a hundred-hectare fragment. It covered nearly half a square mile. Picking our way through the edge, we came into the magical cathedral gloom of deep rain forest. Choirs of birds sang from a many-layered canopy. Smooth-barked emergents 20 feet around rose a hundred feet before branching, then soared another hundred feet to lord over the forest, providing perches for toucans and parrots. Stilt-root trees stood on their strange scaffolding. On the forest floor, husks of nuts, fruits, and beans testified to the rich larder supporting rain forest biodiversity.

Dr. Stouffer pointed toward the fragment center: "I hear a mixed-species flock." We moved quietly. Soon small birds of all descriptions flitted around us, led by an antshrike. "There could be 20 species in this flock—this is what you don't see in the smaller fragments." Butterflies fluttered at flowering trees, among them the flashing neon blue morpho. "Jaguarundi and margay may be in here," said Dr. Stouffer. "Hunters seek them. For the larger animals, I believe hunting is more of a threat than the cutting."

For many groups seeking to protect biodiversity, a promising strategy is that of extractivism—of sustainably harvesting non-timber products from the standing forest. It is based on the tenet that the living, intact forest is too valuable to cut down for a one-time timber harvest.

Extractivism has thrived for centuries in the vast forests of Southeast Asian nations. In Amazonia, the effort to foster extractivism is highly politicized. It pits powerful cattle and development interests against the growing power of forest peoples, including Indians, and their worldwide supporters. In Brazil, arguing the case for the forests has proved dangerous. The 1988 murder of activist rubber tapper Chico Mendes is the most infamous of perhaps scores of assassinations of forest leaders.

The heyday of extraction in Brazil was the rubber boom. Before cultivated rubber achieved dominance early in this century, the tapping of wild rubber trees employed 150,000 laborers, stimulated exploration of Amazonia to the headwaters of every major river, and built the prosperous inland port of Manaus. Today the harvesting of Brazil nuts leads among nontimber forest industries. Fifty million dollars' worth of nuts a year flow by freighter from Belém to foreign ports.

The question of how much wealth can be sustainably harvested from the Amazon rain forest fuels part of the debate swirling around extractivism. In 1989 three highly respected botanists published a study showing that harvests of available fruits, nuts, and latex from Peruvian Amazonia would, over the long term, yield more than ten times the value of the most intelligent cutting of the trees themselves.

The report stirred a hornets' nest. Timber interests claimed exaggerations. Others claimed that the forest around Iquitos, where the study was made, is among the most productive in Amazonia, and thus atypical of rain forests in general. Many economic ecologists take a middle ground. They see extractivism as a limited, though important tool among several that can contribute toward the preservation of rain forest ecosystems.

# A testing ground

In the western state of Acre, home of the slain Chico Mendes, I began my visit with a call on one of his official heirs, the head of the rubber tappers' union. The union headquarters occupied a modest former home in the state capital of Rio Branco, a frontier town where guests in the largest hotel can be awakened in the morning by the crowing of cocks.

"The forest people have always lost land through the violence of intruders, and by gullibly selling their rights for small sums," said Julio Barbosa de Aquino, himself a tapper—short, muscular, drumming the wooden floor with a foot as he waited for an assistant to translate into English. "Now the government has set aside two large forest areas as extractive reserves here in Acre. More have been designated in other Amazonian states. The reserves' legal status is not secure, but when it is they will protect our rights as long as we protect the forest.

"The union has two objectives—to find good markets for diversified products of the rain forest, and to improve the quality of what we sell." I knew that discouraging comments abound about rubber being poorly processed in the forest, harvested Brazil nuts turning rancid, and gatherers not meeting contract schedules with buyers.

A concerted international effort makes Acre a test-tube case for saving forest biodiversity through extractivism. Leadership comes from the Ford Foundation and other organizations. Much of their work centers on a workers' cooperative for processing and marketing Brazil nuts located in the remote town of Xapuri, where Chico Mendes was assassinated.

Accompanied by interpreter Rosa Maria Roldan of the rubber tappers' union, I rented a car and driver and set forth from Rio Branco toward Xapuri on a road that in reality was a hundred-mile succession of potholes. Ms. Roldan accepted the roughness with approval. "If they pave the road," she said, "the loggers and cattlemen will come and push down the virgin forest. The wood will go to Japan. The forest people will lose out."

I saw that much forest already had fallen to broad pasture grazed by humped, cloud-gray Zebu cattle. The driver spoke and pointed out the window. Ms. Roldan explained: "We are passing (Continued on page 168)

Taking inventory, parataxonomists gather insect and plant specimens in Costa Rica's rain forest. The country, smaller than West Virginia, harbors as many as 500,000 species of flora and fauna, most unclassified by science. Any of the untested organisms could contain the raw material for a new wonder drug, organic pesticide, or other beneficial agent worth millions of dollars. To turn such natural wealth into cash without destroying the living source is a goal of a landmark program run by

Costa Rica's National Institute of Biodiversity, or INBio. The effort includes labeling millions of samples, such as columnea (opposite, top), in the hope of eventually cataloging, studying, and preserving all the country's plants and animals.

FOLLOWING PAGES: Costa Rica's golden beetles—two species are shown here—commonly display variation within a single species, a trait of adaptation that underlies the origin of biological diversity.

*Union leader Osmarino Amâncio Rodrigues holds a picture of his predecessor, Amazonia's eco-martyr Chico Mendes. Mendes helped create the first union of forest workers—the rubber tappers—and campaigned passionately to save the rain forest. Ranchers—or their gunmen—intent on clearing parts of western Amazonia fatally shot Mendes in 1988.*

*Ants arch in front of Harvard's Edward O. Wilson, the dean of biodiversity studies. Wilson places the number of living species known today at 1.4 million. Change threatens this diversity, along with millions of organisms yet to be named. He warns of "a new period of mass extinction…coming from human pressure on the environment."*

the world's largest cemetery for Brazil nut trees." I saw them—enormous solitary trees, miles of them, spaced a few hundred yards apart, many mere standing skeletons, many reaching out with branches obviously dying. "The law forbids cutting Brazil nut trees, so the ranchers fell everything around them, and then burn the pasture each year. Of course the trees die."

We approached Xapuri and the Brazil nut cooperative. "It began in the mid-1980s, when Chico Mendes went among the rubber tappers and persuaded them to start a co-op for selling their rubber and buying supplies," explained Ms. Roldan. "The people realized they could do the same with Brazil nuts. In 1990 they opened the nut-processing plant, and it grew into today's factory, with 240 members."

We entered the co-op office, on the banks of the chocolate Acre River. Manager Mario Jorge Fadel showed me the rubber storehouse, with its small stacks of latex pods; the supply warehouse, stocked with flour and beans and flashlight batteries; the samples of products marketing the Brazil nuts: Fruit and Nut Mix, Cashew Crunch, Rainforest Crunch, Rainforest Crisp, all in biodegradable bags. Most bore a label noting that the proceeds helped protect the rain forest, and that 30 percent of the profits were being donated to Cultural Survival, Inc., which located the markets.

The co-op manager looked worried. Had I noticed a green truck toiling along the road to Xapuri? The factory had a large stockpile of processed nuts ready for shipment, and if the truck did not arrive soon to carry them to refrigeration, they would turn rancid. The truck sometimes broke down on the road—a penalty of the potholes.

A wiry, gregarious man strode in—a rubber tapper and union leader. Long ago, Francisco Ramalho de Souza's great-grandparents and

many of their countrymen had fled drought-stricken northeastern Brazil and entered the forest to become tappers. His grandparents, as children, had Indian playmates, and his grandmother married an Indian. Now he had planted 5,000 rubber trees and was teaching agroforestry to other union members—which fruit and nut trees to plant, how to graft trees, what seeds were best for Acre's soils, diseases, and insect pests.

We visited the nut-processing factory, a steel-roofed structure. Inside rose small mountains of plastic sacks bulging with nuts. The supervisor approached, a grizzled part-time rubber tapper. He led us through the processing: nuts soaking in tanks; 40 women in hairnets sorting the nuts for size and cracking the shells in little vises; shell-fired ovens cooking the nuts for 24 hours. Many employees sampled nuts as they worked, including the supervisor: "I eat them all day when I'm in the forest, too."

A corner of the building held 27 tons of processed nuts, sealed in bags and boxed. The green truck—when it arrived—would take them to distant Pôrto Velho in Rondônia; a river boat to Manaus; another ship to the United States. There, they and other forest plants would become ingredients in Ben & Jerry's ice cream, Body Shop oils, and other products.

We departed the factory for a short trip down a street of small houses in Xapuri. The last house on the left wore aqua blue paint, pink shutters, and the cooling shade of a huge *apuirana* tree. The house bore the number 487 and a sign: *"Centro de Memória Chico Mendes."*

For days, gunmen had lain in wait in bushes behind, near the outhouse. Chico Mendes emerged from the back porch, wrapped in a towel, to be ripped by 60 pellets from a 20-gauge shotgun. That year, seven other political murders stained central Acre.

# Buttonholing the rain forest

The effort to promote nontimber rain forest products enjoys growing consumer appeal and a certain chic. An example is the engaging Tagua Initiative of Conservation International. It began when Mark Plotkin, ruminating on rampant destruction of Ecuadorean forests and diversity, recalled the one-time popularity of buttons made from the ivory-like nut of Ecuador's tagua palm. Plastics had crowded out tagua and, with it, a profitable extractive industry in the vanishing western Andean rain forest.

To revive the industry, Conservation International established a partnership with two major purveyors of trendy clothing. Together they would purchase the raw materials for a million tagua buttons from forest providers and pay licensing fees to support CI's biodiversity programs. Since then, more than 30 other companies have joined in, offering clothes that sometimes bear the tag, "Wear a Piece of the Rain Forest." Today villagers in coastal Ecuador are shipping 20 to 40 tons of nuts a month to local button factories.

In 75 countries, 300 biosphere reserves established under the auspices of UNESCO seek to demonstrate that human activities—including economic development—can take place beside conservation and scientific research without violence to the environment.

The concept faces daunting challenges in Guatemala. The Maya Biosphere Reserve covers some three and a half million acres of tropical forest in Guatemala. Combined with the neighboring forests in Mexico and Belize, this region formed the heartland of the ancient Maya civilization. The reserve also is a magnet for land-ravenous peasants who crowd nearby uplands.

"The pressures are incredible, and building," said anthropologist James Nations of CI, who spent three years with the neighboring Lacandon Indians in Mexico. "Population growth is such that in 20 years there'll be two people where there is one today, wanting to cut down trees to grow corn. We've got to help them meet their needs with alternatives. The only guy who can practice conservation is the one on the spot, with the ax."

To provide these alternatives, a program sponsored by the U. S. Agency for International Development harnesses the skills of three U. S. environmental groups. CI promotes the harvesting of three abundant forest resources: chicle, the tree resin used as a base for chewing gums; allspice, the valued seasoning; and a decorative leaf from the xate palm, prized as a backdrop for flower arrangements. CARE encourages environmental education and reforestation. The Nature Conservancy conducts training in managing the reserve.

The Maya Biosphere Reserve is the beneficiary of another strategy for protecting biodiversity: ecotourism. Ruins of the ancient civilization abound in the reserve, among them the famous temples at Tikal. Already tourists spend 25 million dollars a year in the reserve area, and the potential is much larger. "Done correctly," said Karen Ziffer of CI, "ecotourism can bring in foreign exchange and support restaurants, hotels, T-shirt shops. The trick is to do it right—to observe the area's carrying capacity, and to be sure the money stays with the residents of the forest."

As with the search for medicinal plants, the protection of priceless wild agricultural strains has involved narrow escapes from extinction. A classic case involves a relative of corn, which, like all modern monocultures, is nerve-rackingly vulnerable to disease.

In the 1970s, a Mexican college student discovered a new species of corn, *Zea diploperennis*, in the state of Jalisco. Research revealed that it carried genetic resistance to nine corn viruses, one of which poses a threat to U. S. hybrids. The species also is the only known corn to be a perennial. The narrow escape: The new corn was confined to an area of less than 25 acres and grew in the path of farmers clearing and burning the land. It was discovered only a week before the arrival of machete and fire.

USAID projects are far-flung. The agency's 1993 preliminary report on environmental programs makes clear the need in sub-Saharan Africa:

Environmental indicators for Africa's agriculture, forestry, and wildlife continue to slide downward. Per capita food production has declined by 5 percent over the last decade. Sub-Saharan Africa has the world's highest population growth, more than 3 percent a year. Five million hectares of forest—an area half the size of South Carolina—are cleared each year. Soils are degraded on more than one-fifth of Africa's arable land. Wildlife populations have declined precipitously in recent years.

A scattering of USAID's African biodiversity projects includes elephant conservation in Niger, Cameroon, Tanzania, Botswana, Zambia, Kenya, and Zimbabwe; increasing the effectiveness of some 200 African conservation organizations; the promotion of national environmental action plans in beleaguered countries such as Madagascar and Rwanda; the preservation of parklands through support of park-edge communities; the eventual protection of a vast forested area shared by Cameroon, the Central African Republic, and the Congo; groundwork toward protecting the unique fish fauna of Lake Tanganyika, threatened by sediments; tree planting in Senegal to fight desertification.

I turned homeward to ask: How fares biological diversity in the United States? Thousands of species of plants and animals are under stress, some acutely so. Some species once on the brink now ride the comeback trail. For most that ail or once ailed, the problem is our disruption of their habitat: destruction of wetlands through filling and draining; transformation of land by agriculture, grazing, and logging; paving by development.

For those plants and animals forced to the edge of the abyss, the safety net is the federal Endangered Species Act. It is a powerful instrument. When a concerned party submits a candidate species to the Fish and Wildlife Service or the National Marine Fisheries Service, and the lengthy screening procedures are successfully completed, the act mobilizes sweeping legal and administrative remedies—witness the spotted owl.

Since passage of the act in 1973, about 800 species within the United States have been listed as either endangered—at imminent risk of extinction—or as threatened—at risk of moving into endangered status. Only seven species once listed as endangered have recovered and been removed from the list: the Pacific gray whale, the Atlantic coast's brown pelican, the American alligator, three species of South Pacific birds, and a plant, the Rydberg's milk-vetch of the northern Rockies.

# Judging the numbers

The low rate of recovery invites criticism that the act has failed. "The numbers look bad," agreed Michael Bean, a legal specialist with the Environmental Defense Fund. "But they are not the best standard for judging the act. The larger point is that many listed species are showing definite signs of recovery.

"About a dozen have been reclassified from endangered to threatened, including several western fish and the Utah prairie dog. Some species still listed as endangered are coming back, including the bald eagle and peregrine falcon. Others on the list have been reintroduced, such as the red wolf and black-footed ferret. Still others have seen a halt in their decline, or a slowing decline.

"A principal reason for the low rate of recovery," emphasized Mr. Bean, "is that many plants and animals are not listed until their populations are so low as to be hanging in the balance." An EDF study led by ecologist David Wilcove showed that of 492 species listed or proposed between 1985 and 1991, the median number of surviving individual animals was only about a thousand, and of plants about a hundred. A major problem is that the listing agencies lack the staff for timely analysis of the more than 3,000 candidate applications awaiting determination.

Instead of spreading a net for species at the brink, can we work back and protect them in their habitat? Such a switch, from endangered species to endangered ecosystems, would avoid the crisis management inherent in today's approach.

This is the thrust of a bold new program of the Sierra Club, launched in celebration of the centennial of its founding by naturalist John Muir in 1892. "With the help of staff biologists and a lot of outside experts," said campaign director William Meadows, "we identified 21 critical ecoregions in the United States and Canada. Task forces for each region looked at the threats to biodiversity—in some cases logging, in others agriculture, even air or water quality. Then they drew up plans to resolve these threats. Now we're raising the funds to mobilize grassroots support for legislative action. The Sierra Club is essentially a political organization, able to work for conservation at the level of the state house, Congress, the White House.

"The idea is to protect ecosystems as a whole. Then species can take care of themselves."

This concept has taken hold at the federal level. Bruce Babbitt, Secretary of the Interior, took a first step in an ecosystem-protection approach by setting up a national biological survey under the leadership of two renowned conservationists, Thomas Lovejoy and Dr. Peter H. Raven, the director of the Missouri Botanical Garden. Their mapping will produce a computerized picture of the nation's biodiversity. That picture will be used to guide development along paths least disruptive to fragile habitats— the great need of biodiversity in a world of mounting human pressures.

*Victims of human abuse: How this Alaskan bald eagle ran afoul of a halibut hook remains a mystery. Perhaps the raptor impaled itself when it snatched up a fish scrap— discarded hook and all by a careless fisherman. Naturalists removed the barb. Rescue never came for a tiger in Taiwan. In many areas of Asia, a multimillion-dollar folk medicine trade encourages tiger poaching. Many Asians believe that tiger blood and body parts soothe sundry human ills. Widespread illegal slaughter could eradicate tigers by the end of the century.*

*FOLLOWING PAGES: Pachyderms play tug-of-war in a friendly test of strength and status. A worldwide ban on ivory trade has for now saved elephants from extinction.*

# Keys to the FUTURE

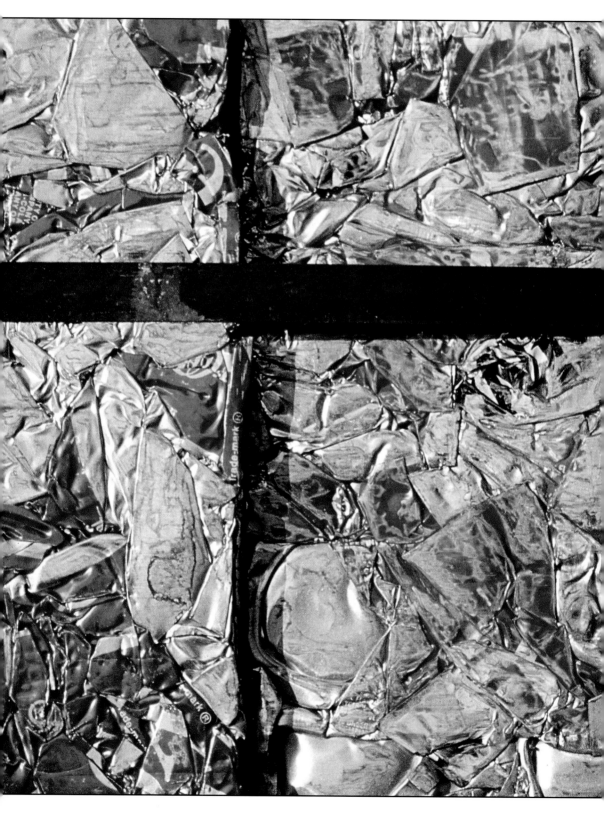

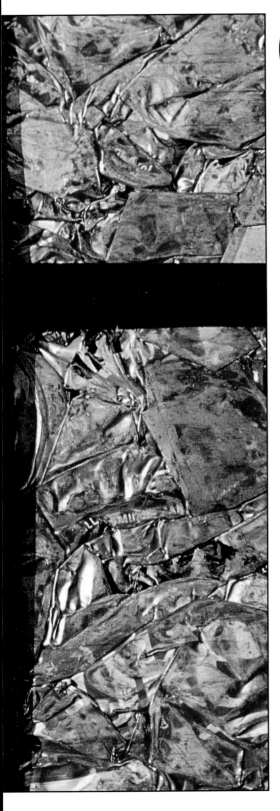

Crushed cans await recycling in
environmentally wise processes
by which, every year, millions of
tons of aluminum and steel are
recovered and reused.

C
an we take a look
ahead, at what we
might expect in coming
years? We can try, prefacing the
effort with a thunderous warning that the astronomical number of variables and uncertain-
ties in such an undertaking make
it a high-risk venture for man,
woman, or supercomputer.

This said, there is one
important truth that all probably
can agree on: The future of
the environment, locally and
planetwide, will be shaped not
so much by sweeping governmental actions but by each of us,
individually, in how we use the
Earth we share. How efficient
our car. How few our trips. How
efficient our light bulbs and our

refrigerator. How careful our farming practices, how controlled our industrial effluents.

"Nobody can do anything to heal a planet," said author and educator Wendell Berry in a memorable 1989 commencement address at the College of the Atlantic in Maine. "The suggestion that anybody could do so is preposterous....

"The question that *must* be addressed...is not how to care for the planet, but how to care for each of the planet's millions of human and natural neighborhoods, each of its millions of small pieces and parcels of land, each one of which is in some precious and exciting way different from all the others.

"Our understandable wish to preserve the planet must somehow be reduced to the scale of our competence—that is, to the wish to preserve all of its humble households and neighborhoods....

"The great obstacle is simply this: the conviction that we cannot change because we are dependent upon what is wrong.

"But that is the addict's excuse, and we know that it will not do."

Our most flagrant environmental addiction is, of course, fossil fuels. The prodigious snorting of oil and coal inflicts ills far more immediate than global warming. It brings polluted air with attendant injuries to forests, crops, and human health; it seeds acid rain; it produces massive trade imbalances; it poses the risks of spill-prone transport in an aging tanker fleet and an increasing dependence on a volatile Middle East; and, in coal mining, it perpetuates the most dangerous major American occupation. Recent efficiencies have reduced the U. S. share of fossil fuels consumption. But the nation still uses them only half as efficiently as trade rivals Germany and Japan, and belches out 24 percent of all fossil-fuel emitted carbon dioxide. It is a costly addiction.

Institutional treatment is ever more available. The effective efficiency programs for electric power utilities, designed by Amory Lovins, midwifed by the Natural Resources Defense Council, and first adopted by the California utilities, are spreading nationwide.

Their architects, meanwhile, are extending their efforts into other sectors that share the fossil fuel addiction: building, industry, and transportation. A strategy outlined in the report *America's Energy Choices*, drawn up by the NRDC, the Alliance to Save Energy, the American Council for an Energy-Efficient Economy, and the Union of Concerned Scientists, would in 40 years reduce the nation's petroleum consumption and $CO_2$ emissions by two-thirds and achieve net savings of some 2.3 trillion dollars.

In the construction industry, for example, the analysts discovered "a tremendous potential for cost-effective energy savings...from the use of more than 60 types of conservation technologies and measures currently available, ranging from more efficient lighting, windows, and appliances in existing residences to more efficient heating, ventilating, and air-conditioning systems in new commercial buildings."

The world's mayors are enlisting in the war against energy waste. Impetus stems from a UN affiliate, the International Council for Local

Environmental Initiatives. The potential is enormous: More than 50 percent of the world's people are urbanites and their number is growing. A leader is Helsinki, Finland, which recycles for district heating the waste heat from power stations and other sources.

The NRDC's Ralph Cavanagh looks to the day when carbon dioxide release will stand as a stigma, a symbol of wasted energy and an uncompetitive economy. "High carbon dioxide emissions should be regarded as a national failure, like high rates of child malnutrition and child illiteracy," said Dr. Cavanagh.

Those concerned with global warming, and with the health of environments such as Chesapeake Bay, see part of the problem in the subsidized cheapness of petroleum products, particularly gasoline. "An obvious way to protect the environment is to levy a gasoline tax," said the University of New Hampshire's Berrien Moore, an expert on the global carbon cycle. "European nations tax gasoline a dollar or two, and we don't see their economies failing because of it."

# Guardians of the forests

Just as the world shows unease about the global effects of burning fossil fuels, it shares a concern for the tropical forests and their irreplaceable wealth of biological diversity. What can be done? If forests are preserved, how are we obligated to those who preserve them for us?

In the rain forest north of Manaus in Brazil I visited a promising agroforestry project sponsored by North Carolina State University and the Brazilian agricultural department. As I was departing, researcher João Carlos de Souza Matos spoke a thought that had weighed on his mind all of that hot day in the field: "I believe the rain forest belongs to the world. And the world must help us preserve it."

Persuasive support for this position comes from a study by a team of U. S. and Brazilian scientists. I heard the message from one of the authors, Daniel C. Nepstad of the Woods Hole Research Center.

"We looked at rubber-tapper families in the Chico Mendes Extractive Reserve in Acre," said Dr. Nepstad. "An average family might control 300 hectares [750 acres] of forest. It clears about 1.5 hectares a year for planting rice, beans, and manioc, releasing 315 tons of stored carbon a year. The family maintains the remainder of the 300 hectares of standing forest for the extraction of rubber, Brazil nuts, and other products. The forest that the family is maintaining stores some 60,000 tons of carbon in its biomass.

"Thus the rubber tappers and other forest residents are acting as guardians of globally significant amounts of carbon. The three million hectares of Brazil's extractive reserves hold an amount of carbon equaling more than 10 percent of the carbon *(Continued on page 184)*

*FOLLOWING PAGES: An ice-cream parlor in Delhi, India, enjoys a booming business. As population grows, Earth's resources face increasing strain. A person in a wealthy nation will, over a lifetime, consume a hundred times the resources of one in a poor country.*

*Family planning around the world: A poster in a Nigerian health clinic (opposite), a billboard in Chengdu, China, and a condom ad blazoned on the sail of a Bangladesh dinghy testify to the increasing urgency of population control in many parts of the world. As Paul Erlich, a demographic expert at Stanford University, explains, "While over-population in poor nations tends to keep them poverty-stricken, over-population in rich nations tends to undermine the life-support capacity of the entire planet." From the time of Christ, it took about 1,700 years for Earth's population to double. Since then, humanity has doubled three times in ever decreasing time spans. Some scientists predict the next doubling—to 10 billion people—by the year 2070.*

released annually by global combustion of fossil fuels." Many benefits of the standing forest, said the study, "accrue to those living outside extractive reserves and outside of Brazil. A fundamental question that Brazilian and global societies need to address is how the beneficiaries will pay for such benefits and who will receive such payments."

Such payments would be useful. The human poverty endemic to much of the tropics, the exploding populations, and the haunting presence of widespread malnutrition stand as probably the greatest threats to vast tropical ecosystems on which those regions depend.

"We will never protect the environment if we focus on it alone," said Patrick Webb of the International Food Policy Research Institute. "Rules about cutting trees or protecting soil will never work as long as people must gather fuelwood and cultivate food. We must look at the parallel problems of poverty and food security. The linkages are too close."

Africa faces the greatest challenge. Observed Dr. Webb: "The roads are not there, markets are not in place or are politically distorted, only 5 percent of the agriculture is irrigated, and there's a lack of institutions for credit, fertilizers, and—most needed—education. Also, in much of Africa, the population growth rate still is ferocious."

The rate of tropical deforestation and other environmental degradation ties in directly to the rate of population growth. Population expert Paul Harrison of the United Kingdom attributes 79 percent of the forest clearing in Third World nations to population pressures. The remainder is divided between cutting for timber and for rain forest ranching.

# The population curve

A recent study of family size in 44 developing countries sees a "reproductive revolution," in which about a third of married women now use modern family planning methods. Contrary to popular belief, the use occurs even among families lacking education or a comfortable standard of living—both long thought to be necessary preconditions for family size reduction. The success would be greater, claims the UN Fund for Population Activities, if contraceptives could be made available to some 300 million women who want but cannot obtain them.

Thailand shines as a beacon lighting the way to effective population control. Back in the 1960s the Thais reeled under a growth rate of 3.32 percent, one of the world's highest. A worried government reacted in 1970 with a family-planning program that included grassroots campaigns and the provision of temporary and permanent contraceptive methods.

The results restructured Thai demographics and unleashed an economic surge. According to Patama Bhiromrut of the Family Health Division, by 1989 the program had prevented 13 million births. Studies showed that savings in expenditures for education, public health, and other services yielded a 40-fold return on every dollar spent on family planning. "All savings," wrote Dr. Bhiromrut, "have been channeled into economic investment, with the result that economic growth rose sharply...."

Paul Ehrlich of Stanford University, who has dedicated much of an academic career to alerting the world to population dynamics, offers a thoughtful encapsulation of where we stand: "For most of the 3.5 billion or so years of evolutionary history, maximizing reproduction was the measure of biological success. Human beings followed this standard for millions of years. Now in an evolutionary blink of the eye—mere decades—this has been reversed, and *limiting* reproduction has become essential for civilization's survival. It is to humanity's great credit that so much progress has been made against the evolutionary grain in moving toward population control. We may have a long way to go, but we have come a long way fast."

The environmental movement, too, has come a long way. In June 1992 the largest gathering of nations in world history convened under UN auspices in Rio de Janeiro to confront the problems of the environment, and the related need for development. From that historic meeting, and the years of groundwork preceding it, came an ambitious blueprint for reshaping human activities to minimize environmental damage and ensure sustainable development. It is known as Agenda 21—an agenda for steering human development into the 21st century. All of the attending 178 nations, including the United States, signed the three-volume action plan. They represented more than 98 percent of the global population.

Agenda 21 calls for much: eventual eradication of poverty; modifying consumption patterns; raising agricultural productivity without environmental damage; addressing population dynamics; developing water policies and a transition away from fossil fuels; protecting forests and biodiversity; curbing desertification; safely channeling biotechnology into world agriculture and health services; protecting the atmosphere and oceans; and managing wastes and chemicals. It would foster the implementation of these goals in developing nations through improved access to information and technology, heightened technological capacity, and aid from industrial countries that by the year 2000 would amount to 0.7 percent of their gross national product.

As would be expected, compliance with this sweeping program is voluntary for each signatory nation. A survey conducted by the Natural Resources Defense Council a year after Rio showed that 65 countries, including the major ones, had taken limited steps toward implementation.

The Earth Summit in Rio showed deep concern for the world's forests. A statement of 27 principles outlines a global consensus for rights, responsibilities, management, conservation, and sustainable development of forests of all types. The conference produced two international conventions of potentially major impact for the environment, each signed by more than 160 nations. Both were rejected by the U. S. delegation of the Bush Administration and subsequently embraced by that of President Clinton.

One of the conventions—on biodiversity—confronts the emotional issue of pharmaceutical and other firms sharing profits and technology with nations in which they discover useable natural products. The other convention—on climate change—stipulates that industrial nations will aim to reduce greenhouse gas emissions to 1990 levels by the year 2000.

Controlling $CO_2$ to meet the terms of the convention on climate

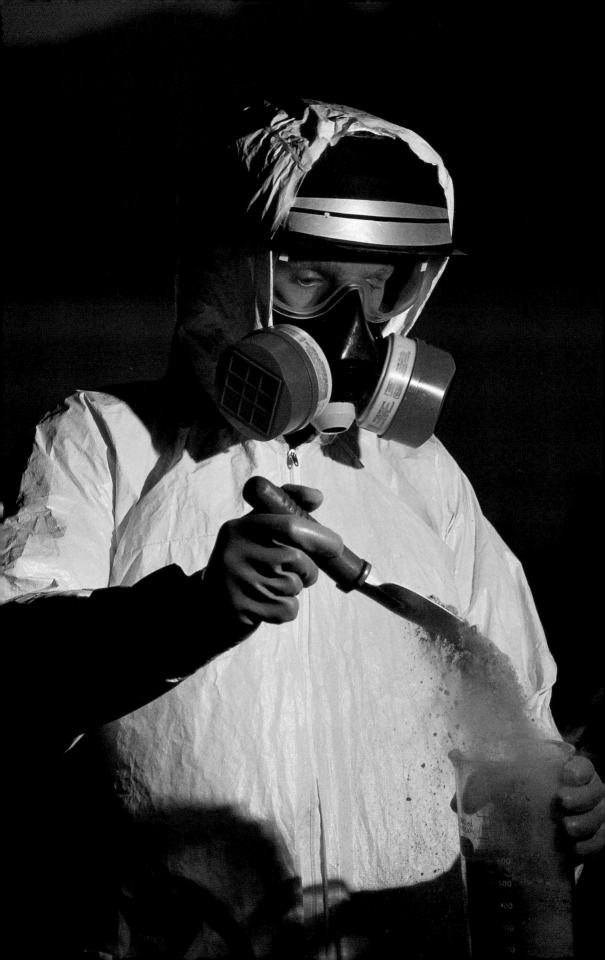

*For some two billion years before higher life-forms evolved, nature's recyclers, bacteria, pioneered life on Earth. These oil-eating bacteria, pseudomonas putida (below), are related to those genetically engineered in 1972 to help clean up oil spills and soil contaminated by leaking storage tanks. Today, in a booming new technology, some 50 companies in the U. S. put microbes to work to help detoxify or neutralize man-made messes. A technician dressed in mask, goggles, gloves, and protective suit, takes a soil sample from an industrial storage site polluted by leakage. Bacteria and yeasts have long been used to produce foods such as bread and yogurt. Now scientists are devising ways to use these organisms to help clean up the environment.*

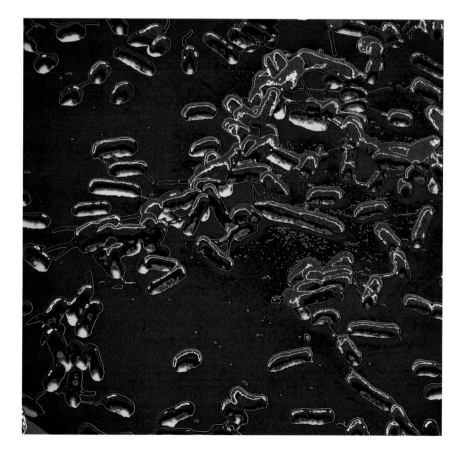

could be good news for the world's forests. The vehicle is a win-win strategy called carbon offset. When Applied Energy Services of Arlington, Virginia, set about building a coal-fired power plant for a Connecticut utility, it simultaneously contributed two million dollars to plant 52 million trees in heavily deforested Guatemala, in a project conducted by CARE. During the projected 40-year lifespan of the power plant, the trees will take up an estimated 80 percent of the amount of carbon dioxide it exhales.

In another offset arrangement, New England Electric System of Massachusetts neutralizes some of the millions of tons of $CO_2$ it emits each year by introducing scientific forestry techniques to the cutting of rain forest in Malaysia. By carefully extracting the trees, trained loggers can leave 50 tons more carbon standing per hectare cut.

Current U. S. offset programs could be the vanguard of a mass movement. "The forest-management and tree-planting programs have taken up more carbon than expected," said Kenneth Andrasko of the EPA, "and the programs appear to be highly cost effective. Several states already require carbon offset of new generating capacity, and voluntary action and regulation could spread. Hundreds of millions of hectares in the tropics are available for planting, so the potential is enormous."

Prodigious activity focuses on protecting the world's forests, and with them, biodiversity. I saw a hint of this groundswell at an annual meeting of the International Society of Tropical Foresters. Members crowded into a small auditorium in Washington, D. C. One by one they stood and explained their missions. The Pan American Development Foundation works in Haiti with nongovernmental organizations to plant barren hillsides with trees for fuelwood, fodder, green manure, windbreaks, and as barriers to catch and hold the eroding soil. Similar programs exist in El Salvador, Costa Rica, and on three Caribbean islands. Indonesia conducts an ambitious program of reforestation, sustainable forestry, and fire-damage control. The Society of American Forestry pursues research into sustained forest productivity, biodiversity, and the relationship between forests and ground water. The New Forest Project distributes free seeds in bulk for agroforestry and reforestation and trains those who burn fuelwood to use efficient cookers.

In addition, the World Conservation Union has farflung forest conservation programs, while the Tropical Forest Foundation, a rare coalition of conservation and industrial interests, disseminates information and stresses proper use of the forests. The U. S. Agency for International Development sponsors nearly a hundred forestry projects around the world, in partnership with organizations such as CARE, World Wildlife Fund, the Nature Conservancy, World Learning, and Conservation International.

Like the forests, other key areas of environmental concern enjoy strong and active global constituencies. The financial resources of these efforts are substantial and growing. The human resources are unmatched— legions of workers of all ages, dedicated, driven, and often highly professional. In developing nations, the tens of thousands of nongovernmental organizations contend with local problems that include the environment.

Is the environmental movement up to the colossal task at hand?

While the answer will come only with time, an impression grew on me during my coverage for this book—a feeling that a somewhat similar drama had played on the world stage two decades ago, and could offer an analogy to today's challenges and responses.

World hunger was the issue in those early 1970s—global food-stocks perilously depleted, drought and famine scourging the Sahel, pockets of starvation tormenting India, world population soaring—in short, all of the precursors of Malthusian doom. Worst off was Bangladesh, 85 million cramming a land the size of Wisconsin, hunger endemic, starvation common, and hope hard to find. Gaunt forms crowded everywhere, silent and uncomplaining. Bangladesh was thought hopeless. Many wrote it off, and it was difficult not to agree.

In that time of hardship, however, the world turned out to help. Traveling the stricken land back then, I counted some 70 relief organizations working hard and patiently to improve agriculture with new crops, livestock, and expanded irrigation, to instill family planning, to strengthen education and health services.

Today Bangladesh bulges with some 112 million inhabitants—close to half the population of the United States crammed into that Wisconsin-size land. But they are reasonably well fed, and almost entirely by their own efficient food production. The population growth rate has declined sharply. Credit for this resurrection rests on the agricultural skill of the Bangladeshis, wise government policies, and—in ways admittedly difficult to measure—the success of that outpouring of help.

# A global parallel

A similar outpouring now focuses on the environment. True, the environment is global. But so is the outpouring. Can environmental ills, like our medical ills, be reduced by *preventative* measures? Of course they can. The need is pressing, the opportunity vast.

"The smartest move we can make," explained oceanographer Sylvia Earle, "is to protect what we have, rather than despoil it and face a salvage job. Cleaning up costs a thousand times as much as day-to-day maintenance. Look at the cost of Superfund."

Observed William Eichbaum of the World Wildlife Fund, "At present we make a decision to grow or manufacture something—and only later do we try to cope with the wastes. This mentality must change. We've got to design in the waste handling at the start, and at every stage of a process. The DuPont Company is doing this, with its pledge of zero-discharge of carcinogens by the year 2000. We're at the threshold, and that's better than not knowing where the door is."

Young people are finding that door, in droves. It opened a crack

*FOLLOWING PAGES: Stepping away from Earth gives astronauts a global perspective on the planet's environmental problems. Here, the tendrils of a circular storm system swirl beyond a satellite poised for deployment in the cargo bay of the space shuttle* Discovery.

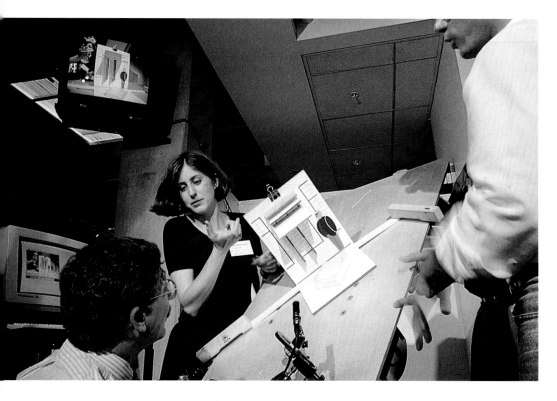

*Designers at Pacific Gas & Electric's Pacific Energy Center in San Francisco use a heliodon to simulate the daily and seasonal passage of sunlight around a building. The device combines an adjustable table, representing Earth, with a ceiling-mounted light source. It helps planners site and design buildings for the best energy efficiency.*

on that first Earth Day in 1970, and each year more enter. Momentum derives from efforts such as the National Geographic Society's Kids Network, an educational television program that encourages interaction on such subjects as acid rain and clean water.

Environmentalism is entering the workplace. "We're trying to bring concern for the environment to the level of today's concern for safety," said Peter Melhus of Pacific Gas and Electric. "Safety is a message that has reached home. Environment isn't there yet, but it can make it. Decades ago you heard complaints that safety rules would break a company. You don't now, but you hear that about environmental regulations. We've got to spread the word that much of what companies do to harm the environment is actually an indicator of waste and inefficiency—that there's money to be saved in being environmental."

Recently I bought some compact fluorescent bulbs, which use 87 percent less electricity than the old incandescents and last ten times longer. I installed one at my word processor station, and started saving about 20 dollars a year—enough to pay for the bulb. Better yet, that single efficient bulb reduced my carbon dioxide release by about 575 pounds a year.

*On a 900-mile-long PG&E pipeline project to bring Canadian gas to central California, crewmen check flashcards to acquaint themselves with wildlife habitats on the route.*

*FOLLOWING PAGES: Hope for the future: Fourth graders from a Marietta, Georgia, school learn the value of small watersheds through their Adopt-A-Stream program.*

Little victories. We're winning more and more. And the grateful Earth feels them, and even records them. One archive for this environmental ledger is the great Greenland ice cap, where each year's snows lay down a record of the pollution of the air through which they fell—powerful proof that what each one of us does makes a difference in our planet's health.

"The ice trapped the history of the Earth's environmental past in air bubbles and dust particles and held it for us to rediscover," explained Paul A. Mayewski of the University of New Hampshire, leader of a team of U. S. scientists who drilled through 200,000 years of accumulated snow layers.

"The rise of the industrial age left a vivid record in the ice. Acid rain shows up in the 1880s, the earliest sign. A sharp rise in carbon dioxide begins in the 1930s—heavier industrialization. We also see the dust bowl of the 1930s, the atomic bomb tests of the 1940s and '50s, the eruption of Mount Saint Helens in 1980, the radioactive fallout from Chernobyl in 1986.

"We see something else. Starting in the 1970s there's a *decrease* in sulfates. The ice clearly records the effect of the Clean Air Act of 1970."

The message of the ice: We *can* change Earth for the better.

## NOTES ON THE AUTHOR

Award-winning writer Thomas Y. Canby turned arcane subjects of science into easy-to-understand adventure for a global audience during his 35 years as a NATIONAL GEOGRAPHIC journalist. His incisive articles won wide recognition, including the Westinghouse-AAAS award and honors fom the National Association of Science Writers. Tom retired in 1991 as the magazine's Senior Assistant Editor, Science, and immediately went to work as a free-lance writer.

## ACKNOWLEDGMENTS

The Book Division wishes to thank the individuals, groups, and organizations named or quoted in the text. In addition, we are especially grateful to Michael Bailey, Michael Edesses, David Harcharik, Russell Mittermeier, Berrien Moore III, Daniel Nepstad, John Perry, Frederick J. Swanson, Mickey Trichel, Paul Uhlir, Stephen Vosti, and Richard S. Williams, Jr.

## ILLUSTRATIONS CREDITS

Photographer James A. Sugar, associated with the Black Star agency, has specialized in a variety of science and technology assignments for the National Geographic Society.

Front Matter: 1- Pekka Parviainen/DEMBINSKY PHOTO ASSOCIATES; 2-3 SOVFOTO/TASS; 4-5 Stephen Frink/WATERHOUSE; 6-7 ANIMALS ANIMALS/EARTH SCENES/E. R. Degginger.

A PLANET UNDER PRESSURE: 8-9 Jim Richardson; 12-13 James A. Sugar/BLACK STAR; 14-15 Fritz Pölking/PETER ARNOLD, INC.; 16-17 Stephanie Maze/WOODFIN CAMP & ASSOCIATES; 18-19 Gerd Ludwig; 22 James A. Sugar/BLACK STAR; 23 James A. Sugar/BLACK STAR and Kevin S. Schumacher; 28-29 David Cavagnaro.

THE EVOLVING ENVIRONMENT: 30-31 Scott T. Smith; 34 Sam Abell; 36-37 Ben Osborne; 38-39 George Steinmetz; 39 (lower left) Colin Milkins/OXFORD SCIENTIFIC FILMS; 39 (lower right) Jacob Mosser III/POSITIVE IMAGES; 42 (upper) T.A. Wiewandt/WILD HORIZONS; 42 (center) Louis Psihoyos/MATRIX; 42 (lower) Lopez de Bertodano/COMSTOCK, INC.; 42-43 Sam Abell; 47 Jonathan S. Blair; 50-51 Greg Vaughn.

THE AIR WE BREATHE: 52-53 Grant V. Faint/THE IMAGE BANK; 56 Robert Winslow; 58-59 Michael Gover/IMPACT; 60 Larry Lee/WESTLIGHT 61 (upper) George Steinmetz; 61 (lower) Richard Olsenius; 62-63 Oliver Strewe/TONY STONE IMAGES; 63 (upper) Merrell Wood/THE IMAGE BANK; 66 Kevin Schafer & Martha Hill; 67 David Robert Austen; 70 Ted Spiegel/BLACK STAR; 70-71 Stephen P. Alexander; 74-75 Josh Mitchell/PROFILES WEST; 76 James A. Sugar/BLACK STAR and Kevin S. Schumacher; 78-79 Bruce Dale, National Geographic Photographer; 79 (all) James A. Sugar/BLACK STAR; 82 (upper) Otto Rogge/THE STOCK MARKET; 82 (lower) Paul Chesley/ PHOTOGRAPHERS ASPEN; 84-85 Ron Sanford/BLACK STAR.

THE FACE OF THE EARTH: 86-87 Gary Benson/COMSTOCK, INC.; 90-91 Scott T. Smith; 92 Steve McCurry; 94 Tom & Pat Leeson/DRK PHOTO; 95 Steven C. Wilson; 98-99 Charles O'Rear; 100-101 (all) James A. Sugar/BLACK STAR; 103 Joseph B. Brignolo/THE IMAGE BANK; 104-105 J. Kyle Keener/MATRIX; 108 Greg Vaughn; 109 Jürgen Vogt/THE IMAGE BANK; 114 Annie Griffiths Belt; 115 Raymond Gehman; 116-117 Nicole Duplaix/PETER ARNOLD, INC.

A WORLD OF WATER: 118-119 Kelvin Aitken/PETER ARNOLD,

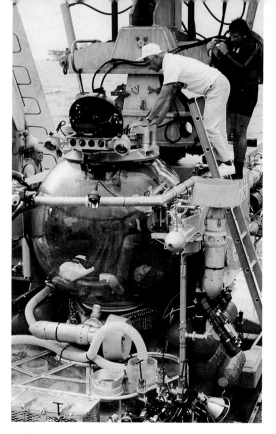

*Author Tom Canby (foreground) examines the* **Johnson SeaLink I,** *the submersible craft that carried him to the floor of the Gulf of Mexico to study bacteria.*

INC.; 122 Bob Cranston; 123 (upper) Al Giddings/OCEAN IMAGES; 123 (lower) Flip Nicklin; 124-125 John Eastcott & Yva Momatiuk; 126-127 (upper) Michael Baytoff; 126 (center) Michael Baytoff; 126 (lower) Greg Vaughn; 126-127 (lower) Cameron Davidson/COMSTOCK, INC.; 128-129 Kelvin Aitken/FIRST LIGHT; 129 Fred Ward/BLACK STAR; 132-133 Bob Sacha; 133 Paul Baumann, U.S. FISH AND WILDLIFE SERVICE; 134-135 Georg Gerster/COMSTOCK, INC.; 138 Jim Olive/PETER ARNOLD, INC.; 139 Natalie Fobes; 142-143 Hromi Naito/URSUS; 143 (both) Natalie Fobes; 144 Amy K. Deputy; 145 Bruce Wodder/THE IMAGE BANK; 146-147 George Grall.

THE WEB OF DIVERSITY: 148-149 Frans Lanting/MINDEN PICTURES; 152-153 Kevin Schafer; 155 Will & Deni McIntyre/PHOTO RESEARCHERS; 156 (upper) David Stone/VISUALS UNLIMITED; 156 (lower) B&C Alexander; 157 Lynn Johnson; 160-161 Mark W. Moffett; 160 (upper and upper center) Kevin Schafer; 160 (lower center) Eugene Fisher; 160 (lower) Gerry Ellis; 164 (upper) Gary Braasch; 164 (lower) Stephen Ferry/MATRIX; 164-165 Stephen Ferry/MATRIX; 166-167 Stephen Ferry/MATRIX; 168 Carlos Humberto/CONTACT PRESS IMAGES; 169 Geoffrey Clifford/WOODFIN CAMP & ASSOCIATES; 172 Tsai Ming Te/ONE EARTH FOUNDATION; 173 Randy Brandon/THIRD EYE PHOTOGRAPHY; 174-175 William E. Thompson.

KEYS TO THE FUTURE: 176-177 Shoji Yoshida/THE IMAGE BANK; 180-181 Dilip Metha/CONTACT PRESS IMAGES; 182 Paul Harrison/PANOS PICTURES; 183 (upper) Richard McCaig/IMPACT; 183 (lower) Trygve Bolstad/PANOS PICTURES; 186 Eugene Fisher; 187 Manfred Kage/PETER ARNOLD, INC.; 190-191 From the IMAX film "Blue Planet"/SMITHSONIAN INSTITUTION/LOCKHEED CORPORATION; 192 and 193 James A. Sugar/BLACK STAR; 194-195 Peter Essick; 196 Emory Kristof, National Geographic Photographer; 200 P. F. Bentley/BLACK STAR.

# Index

**Boldface indicates illustrations.**

Library of Congress CIP data

Canby, Thomas Y.

Our changing Earth / by Thomas Y. Canby ; prepared by the Book Division, National Geographic Society, Washington, D. C.
p. cm.
Includes index.
ISBN 0-87044-910-9
1. Environmentalism. 2. Environmental degradation—Citizen participation. 3. Man—Influence on nature. 4. Conservation of natural resources.
I. National Geographic Society (U.S.). Book Division. II. Title
GE195.C36  1994
363.7—dc20                                        93-48536
                                                      CIP

Composition for this book by the National Geographic Society Book Division with the assistance of the Typographic section of National Geographic Production Services, Pre-Press Division. Set in Palatino. Printed and bound by R. R. Donnelley & Sons, Willard, Ohio. Color separations by Graphic Art Service, Inc., Nashville, Tenn.; Penn Colour Graphics, Inc., Huntingdon Valley, Pa.; Lincoln Graphics, Inc., Cherry Hill, N.J.; and Phototype Color Graphics, Pennsauken, N.J.; Dust jacket printed by Miken Systems, Inc., Cheektowaga, N.Y.

# How You Can Help ...

*A San Francisco Zoo conservation parking meter collects change to help purchase and protect endangered habitats. Each nickel "buys" 18 square feet of rain forest.*

Concern for the Earth has increasingly become a vital part of our social fabric. Following is a list of environmental organizations that welcome your interest and support. In addition, you may get in touch with state and local government agencies and citizens' groups. For more information, consult your public library for volumes such as the National Wildlife Federation's *Conservation Directory* and *Earth Care Annual.*

✳ AMERICAN FORESTRY ASSOCIATION
1516 P Street NW, Washington, D. C. 20005
(202) 667-3300

✳ CANADIAN NATURE FEDERATION
453 Sussex Drive, Ottawa, Ontario K1N 6Z4
(613) 238-6154

✳ CANADIAN WILDLIFE FEDERATION
2740 Queensview Drive, Ottawa, Ontario
K2B 1A2
(613) 721-2286

✳ CHESAPEAKE BAY FOUNDATION, INC.
162 Prince George Street
Annapolis, Maryland 21401
(410) 268-8816

✳ CLEAN WATER ACTION
1320 18th Street NW
Washington, D. C. 20036
(202) 457-1286

✳ CONSERVATION INTERNATIONAL
1015 18th Street NW
Washington, D. C. 20036
(202) 429-5660

✳ NATIONAL AUDUBON SOCIETY
700 Broadway
New York, New York 10003
(212) 797-3000

✳ THE SIERRA CLUB
730 Polk Street
San Francisco, California 94109
(415) 776-2211

✳ THE WILDERNESS SOCIETY
900 17th Street NW
Washington, D. C. 20006
(202) 833-2300

✳ WORLD RESOURCES INSTITUTE
1709 New York Avenue NW
Washington, D. C. 20006
(202) 638-6300

✳ WORLDWATCH INSTITUTE
1776 Massachusetts Avenue NW
Washington, D. C. 20036
(202) 452-1999

✳ WORLD WILDLIFE FUND
1250 24th Street NW
Washington, D. C. 20037
(202) 293-4800